M000316287

YAWN!

YAWN!

Bedtime Reading for Insomniacs

Compiled by

Ellen Sue Stern

TEN SPEED PRESS
Berkeley • Toronto

Copyright © 2000 by Ellen Sue Stern
See page 191 for continuation of copyright information.
All rights reserved. No part of this book may be reproduced in any form, except
brief excerpts for the purpose of review, without written permission of the publisher.

Ten Speed Press
Box 7123
Berkeley, California 94707
www.tenspeed.com

Distributed in Australia by Simon & Schuster Australia, in Canada by Ten Speed
Press Canada, in New Zealand by Southern Publishers Group, in South Africa by
Real Books, in Southeast Asia by Berkeley Books, and in the United Kingdom and
Europe by Airlift Book Company.

Cover design: Paul Kepple
Book design: Chris Hall – CHd Graphic Studio

Library of Congress Cataloging-in-Publication Data
available from publisher

ISBN 1-58008-161-4
Printed in Canada
First printing, 2000

1 2 3 4 5 6 7 8 9 10 — 05 04 03 02 01 00

Contents

Introduction

It's 4:28 A.M.—the sixteenth straight night of sleeplessness and I'm going insane. My hopes were high at midnight when I set the alarm, turned off the light, and settled under the covers in the desperate hope of drifting off into that blessed state of oblivion. My first few nights of insomnia were frustrating, but hardly reason for contemplating suicide. I tossed and turned, checked and rechecked the time, turned on CNN Headline News, switched to the Home Shopping Network, read *People* magazine cover to cover, ate sugar pops out of the box, and finally resigned myself to a lousy night's sleep.

I had a lot on my mind. Deadlines loomed, two kids to pack off to camp, a malingering romance, an outstanding root canal bill. . . . How could anyone sleep with that kind of stress?

Week Two I started to panic. My bedtime rituals became more complex: Adjust the pillow exactly so, prop my teddy bear against the headboard, read twelve pages of anything from *Reader's Digest,* turn off the light, turn on the light, log on to the Depressed Jehovah's Witness web site, stumble back to bed and recite the mantra I was given by my hippie boyfriend in college (*aiiiiiiing*—I know you're supposed to keep it secret). Week Three I walked around in a stupor. I consulted a psychic, saw an acupuncturist, read my horoscope, and had my astrological chart done. I bought a snore-no-more pillow and downed Excedrin PM. I listened to Art Bell broadcast from a bunker in Roswell, borrowed a white-sound machine from a friend—bad idea—every tape had some version of water: soothing waves, rushing canyons, trickling waterfalls, provoking endless trips to the bathroom. I considered joining—or starting—Insomniacs Anonymous. As each night stretched into nightmarish infinity, my anxiety progressed to terror. Insomnia was turning me into a chronically crabby jerk.

Each day was worse, as the cumulative effects eroded my normally pleasant personality. I was rude to the sweet young girl at the dry cleaners. I barked at my children and screamed obscenities at the volunteer calling from the American Cancer Society. I was becoming a candidate for road rage. This couldn't go on. What if I never slept again? My career would topple, my friends would abandon me, my ex-husband would sue for child custody. What if I actually lost it—not much of a stretch—seeing as I was already hallucinating. (Remember that *Star Trek* episode when the entire crew except for Data, the android, becomes psychotic due to prolonged sleep deprivation?)

I had to get creative—and fast. I developed a series of mind games aimed to bore or trick myself into falling asleep. Naturally I started with the old favorite, counting sheep. From there, "One Hundred Bottles of Beer on the Wall." I concentrated on counting exercises: How many different beds I've slept in over forty-five years. How many clothes combinations I could come up with in my closet. Every city I've ever shopped at a supermarket in. Counting and naming. Counting and naming. One night, at 3:55 A.M., I tried counting all the people who would come to my funeral if I died (288!). Still awake, I went through the entire cast of *Twin Peaks* in my mind—and when that didn't work, I did what any sane person does: I prayed, made deals with God. Please, God, just let me get eight hours and I'll think about quitting smoking. Please, God, if you let me sleep, I'll clean my drawers and pay my bills on time and never, ever drive on the shoulder of the road—even in rush hour.

My pleas were in vain. And so, on the sixteenth night of this waking nightmare, I gave up. I got out of bed, walked into my office, turned on my computer, and set out to collect the most numbingly boring reading material that maybe, just maybe, could be my nighttime companion in this long and insidious struggle to sleep. This is the result. I've searched for a wide variety of topics just interesting enough to seduce you into turning the page, yet dull and repetitive enough to make you want to put it down. In the process, I've accumulated a virtual candy store of bizarre and eclectic information—who knew that you never trim the roots on beets? How to eat soup from a bowl without handles? That Elvis met secretly with President Nixon to pitch him on being a special agent in the war against drugs (love the irony!). And I met some of the most amazing individuals: Jon Austin, the front guy for Northwest Airlines who takes the heat when 20,000 furious travelers are stranded . . . my new cyber friend, Leah, in Paris, who testifies to her honest-to-god alien encounter.

So I've had a ton of fun. And, I hope, you will too—especially if this doesn't cure your insomnia. If the reading material doesn't knock you out (literally), hopefully the little quizzes, questions, and exercises will do the trick. I can tell you this much: So far, it's working for me. As I read and re-read the words on these pages, all I want is to crawl under the covers. My pillow beckons, my eyelids droop . . . too tired to continue, I leave you with this wish: May the words on these pages either entertain you or bore you to tears and lull you to sleep.

I was told by a reliable source that there are no words in the English language that rhyme with *silver, purple,* or *orange.* When all else fails, I challenge you to come up with one. So far it's put me to sleep several times, and I still haven't come up with a single word.

QUESTION: What does an agnostic, dyslexic insomniac do?
ANSWER: Lie awake all night trying to figure out the meaning of dog.

Elvis Meets Nixon

Most of us know the famous photo of a dazed-looking Elvis shaking hands with a perplexed-looking Richard Nixon. But how about the letter that got him into the White House in the first place? If you somehow manage to make it all the way through the King's torturous prose, you might conclude that Tricky Dick was either a huge fan of "Burnin' Love," or he didn't have a very busy schedule that day. Ⓨ

ON THE MORNING of December 21, 1970, Elvis Presley personally delivered a letter to the northwest gate of the White House. Written on American Airlines stationery, the five-page letter requested a meeting with President Nixon. Presley intended to present the President with a gift of a World War II-era pistol and obtain for himself the credentials of a federal agent in the war on drugs.

The following is a transcription of the letter that Elvis Presley delivered to the White House on December 21, 1970.

Dear Mr. President,

First, I would like to introduce myself. I am Elvis Presley and admire you and have great respect for your office. I talked to Vice President Agnew in Palm Springs three weeks ago and expressed my concern for our country. The drug culture, the hippie elements, the SDS, Black Panthers, etc. do NOT consider me as their enemy or as they call it The Establishment. I call it America and I love it. Sir, I can and will be of any service that I can to help The Country out. I have no concern or Motives other than helping the country out.

So I wish not to be given a title or an appointed position. I can and will do more good if I were made a Federal Agent at Large and I will help out by doing it my way through my communications with people of all ages. First and foremost, I am an entertainer, but all I need is the Federal credentials. I am on this place with Senator George Murphy and we have been discussing the problems that our country is faced with.

Sir, I am staying at the Washington Hotel, Room 505-506-507. I have two men who work with me by the same of Jerry Schilling and Sonny West. I am registered under the name of Jon Burrows. I will be here for as long as it takes to get the credentials of a Federal Agent. I have done an in-depth study of drug abuse and Communist brain-washing techniques and I am right in the middle of the whole thing where I can and will do the most good.

I am Glad to help just so long as it is kept very Private. You can have your staff or whomever call me anytime today, tonight, or tomorrow. I was nominated this coming year one of America's Ten Most Outstanding Young Men. That will be in January 18 in my home town of Memphis, Tennessee. I am sending you the short autobiography about myself so you can better understand this approach. I would love to meet you just to say hello if you're not too busy.

Respectfully,
Elvis Presley

15% & 20% Tip Table

There's nothing more soothing—or dull—than tables of numbers. If lying in bed and doing your multiplication tables isn't doing the trick, give the 15% and 20% tip table a try. Imagine a waiter bringing you a nice cup of hot cocoa, secure in the knowledge that you'll know what to tip him. Ⓨ

Check	15%	20%	Check	15%	20%
$1.00	$.15	.20	$51.00	$7.65	10.20
$2.00	.30	.40	$52.00	7.80	10.40
$3.00	.45	.60	$53.00	7.95	10.60
$4.00	.60	.80	$54.00	8.10	10.80
$5.00	.75	1.00	$55.00	8.25	11.00
$6.00	.90	1.20	$56.00	8.40	11.20
$7.00	1.05	1.40	$57.00	8.55	11.40
$8.00	1.20	1.60	$58.00	8.70	11.60
$9.00	1.35	1.80	$59.00	8.85	11.80
$10.00	1.50	2.00	$60.00	9.00	12.00
$11.00	1.65	2.20	$61.00	9.15	12.20
$12.00	1.80	2.40	$62.00	9.30	12.40
$13.00	1.95	2.60	$63.00	9.45	12.60
$14.00	2.10	2.80	$64.00	9.60	12.80
$15.00	2.25	3.00	$65.00	9.75	13.00

Check	15%	20%	Check	15%	20%
$16.00	2.40	3.20	$66.00	9.90	13.20
$17.00	2.55	3.40	$67.00	10.05	13.40
$18.00	2.70	3.60	$68.00	10.20	13.60
$19.00	2.85	3.80	$69.00	10.35	13.80
$20.00	3.00	4.00	$70.00	10.50	14.00
$21.00	3.15	4.20	$71.00	10.65	14.20
$22.00	3.30	4.40	$72.00	10.80	14.40
$23.00	3.45	4.60	$73.00	10.95	14.60
$24.00	3.60	4.80	$74.00	11.10	14.80
$25.00	3.75	5.00	$75.00	11.25	15.00
$26.00	3.90	5.20	$76.00	11.40	15.20
$27.00	4.05	5.40	$77.00	11.55	15.40
$28.00	4.20	5.60	$78.00	11.70	15.60
$29.00	4.35	5.80	$79.00	11.85	15.80
$30.00	4.50	6.00	$80.00	12.00	16.00
$31.00	4.65	6.20	$81.00	12.15	16.20
$32.00	4.80	6.40	$82.00	12.30	16.40
$33.00	4.95	6.60	$83.00	12.45	16.60
$34.00	5.10	6.80	$84.00	12.60	16.80
$35.00	5.25	7.00	$85.00	12.75	17.00
$36.00	5.40	7.20	$86.00	12.90	17.20
$37.00	5.55	7.40	$87.00	13.05	17.40
$38.00	5.70	7.60	$88.00	13.20	17.60
$39.00	5.85	7.80	$89.00	13.35	17.80
$40.00	6.00	8.00	$90.00	13.50	18.00
$41.00	6.15	8.20	$91.00	13.65	18.20
$42.00	6.30	8.40	$92.00	13.80	18.40
$43.00	6.45	8.60	$93.00	13.95	18.60
$44.00	6.60	8.80	$94.00	14.10	18.80
$45.00	6.75	9.00	$95.00	14.25	19.00
$46.00	6.90	9.20	$96.00	14.40	19.20
$47.00	7.05	9.40	$97.00	14.55	19.40
$48.00	7.20	9.60	$98.00	14.70	19.60
$49.00	7.35	9.80	$99.00	14.85	19.80
$50.00	7.50	10.00	$100.00	15.00	20.00

Sleepercize

Let's say you go out for dinner on Saturday night. You have prime rib, a baked potato, broccoli with hollandaise sauce, two Heineken, and coffee. Your dining partner has breast of chicken, rice pilaf, mixed vegetables, Diet Pepsi, strawberry cheesecake, and decaf. The bill comes to $56.78. The service was fabulous. How much should you tip the waiter?

Stain Removal Guide

When you get sleepy, things get spilled, as anyone who's nodded off with a hot cup of coffee can painfully attest. Try these dandy stain removal tips to pass the time, but please set aside your midnight snack before you do. ✌

WARNING: Always read garment's label for fabric content and to determine if the garment is dry-clean only or wash only

ADHESIVE TAPE, CHEWING GUM, RUBBER CEMENT — Harden surface with ice; scrape with a dull knife. Saturate with a prewash stain remover or cleaning fluid. Rinse, then launder.

BABY FORMULA — Pretreat or soak stain using a product containing enzymes; soak for at least 30 minutes or several hours for aged stains. Launder.

BEVERAGES *(coffee, tea, soft drinks, wine, alcoholic drinks)* — soak stain in cool water. Pretreat with prewash stain remover, liquid laundry detergent, or a paste of powder detergent and water. Launder with the bleach safe for that fabric. Note: Older stains might respond to treatment with an enzyme product, then laundering.

BLOOD — Soak freshly stained garment in cold water for 30 minutes. Rub detergent into any remaining stain. Rinse, then launder. Dried stains should be pretreated or soaked in tepid water with a product containing enzymes, then laundered. Note: If stain remains, rewash, using a bleach that is safe for that fabric.

CANDLE WAX — Harden with ice, then remove surface wax with a dull knife. Place wax stain between clean paper towels and press with a warm iron. Replace paper towels regularly to absorb more wax and to prevent transferring the stain. Place stain face down on clean paper towels. Sponge remaining stain with a pre-wash stain remover or dry-cleaning fluid; blot with paper towels. Let dry, then launder. Note: If any color remains, relaunder with a bleach that is safe for that fabric.

CATSUP/TOMATO SAUCE — Rinse in cold water, then soak in cool water with 1/4 cup detergent per gallon of water. Spray with a prewash product; launder with a bleach that is safe for that fabric.

CHOCOLATE — Treat the stain with a prewash spray or pretreat with a product containing enzymes. If stain remains, relaunder with bleach that is safe for that fabric.

COFFEE, TEA *(plain or with sugar/sweetener)* — Flush stain immediately with cool water if possible, or soak for 30 minutes in cool water. Rub the stain with detergent and launder with bleach that is safe for that fabric.

COFFEE, TEA *(with cream only)* — Sponge stain with a dry-cleaning solvent. Air dry. Rub with detergent, then launder in hottest water safe for that fabric (with bleach that is safe for that fabric). Pretreat or soak older stains with an enzyme product, then launder.

COLLAR/CUFF SOILS — Rub area with a stain stick product and let remain for 30 minutes, or longer for heavy stains; launder.

COSMETICS — Pretreat with stain stick, prewash stain remover, liquid detergent, or a paste of granular detergent or laundry additive and water, or rub with bar soap. Work into dampened stain until outline of stain is gone; rinse. If greasy stain remains, soak in an enzyme product. Rinse and launder.

CRAYON *(few spots)* — Treat the same as for candle wax, or rub dampened stain with bar soap. Launder with hottest water

Tedious Tips

safe for that fabric. Washer load of clothes can be washed in hot water, using a laundry soap (not detergent) plus 1 cup baking soda. If colored stain remains, launder again, using chlorine bleach, if safe for the fabrics. Otherwise, pretreat or soak in a product containing enzyme or an oxygen bleach using hottest water safe for fabric, then launder.

DAIRY PRODUCTS *(milk, cream, ice cream, yogurt, sour cream, cheese, cream soup)* — Pretreat with stain stick or soak in an enzyme presoak product for 30 minutes if stain is new, or several hours for aged stains; launder.

DEODORANTS, ANTIPERSPIRANTS — Treat light stains with a liquid detergent and then launder. Pretreat heavy stains with a prewash stain remover. Allow to stand 5 to 10 minutes. Launder, using an all-fabric bleach.

DYE TRANSFER *(white garment that has picked up bleeding dye from other garment)* — Remove stains with a commercial color remover; launder. If stain remains, launder again with chlorine bleach, if safe for that fabric. For colored fabrics and whites that cannot be chlorine bleached, soak in oxygen bleach or an enzyme presoak product, then launder. Note: Proper sorting before laundering and not allowing wet clothing to stay in washer after cycle is completed helps prevent this type of stain.

EGG — Pretreat with an enzyme product for 30 minutes for new stain, or several hours for aged stains; launder.

FABRIC SOFTENER — Moisten stain and rub with bar soap. Rinse, then launder. If stain remains, sponge area with rubbing alcohol or dry-cleaning solvent. Rinse thoroughly and relaunder.

FINGERNAIL POLISH —Try nail polish remover, but do not use on acetate or triacetate fabrics. Place stain face down on paper towels and flush with remover. Replace paper towels regularly. Repeat until stain disappears; rinse and launder. Some polishes may be impossible to remove.

FRUIT JUICES — Soak garment in cool water. Wash with bleach that is safe for that fabric.

GRASS STAINS — Pretreat with stain stick or soak with an enzyme product. If stain remains, and if safe for dye, sponge stain with alcohol (dilute alcohol with 2 parts water for use on acetate). If stain still remains, launder in hottest water safe for fabrics, with bleach that is safe for that fabric.

GREASE *(motor oil, animal fat, mayonnaise, salad dressing, butter, cooking oil, or car grease)* — Light stains can be pretreated with a spray stain remover, liquid laundry detergent, or a detergent booster. Launder in hottest water safe for fabric. Place heavy stains face down on clean paper towels. Apply cleaning fluid to the back of stain. Replace towels frequently. Let air dry; rinse. Launder in hottest water safe for that fabric.

INK — Test stain with water or dry-cleaning solvent by placing a drop of each on stain. Use method that removes more of the ink. Ball point ink stains can be placed stain face down on white paper towels. Sponge with rubbing or denatured alcohol or dry-cleaning solvent, or rub detergent into stained area. Repeat if some stain remains. Rinse; launder. Drawing ink usually cannot be removed. Try flushing with cold water until pigments are removed; rub liquid detergent into stain; rinse. Repeat process. Soak in warm sudsy water to which 1 to 4 tablespoons of household ammonia per quart of water have been added. Rinse thoroughly. Launder in hottest water safe for that fabric, with bleach safe for the fabric. Felt Tip or India Ink — Usually cannot be removed. Try pouring water through the stain before it dries, until pigments are removed. Allow to dry. If you notice some reduction in stain, sponge with dry-cleaning solvent. Allow to dry. Rub liquid household cleaner into stain. Rinse. Soak stain (possibly overnight) in warm water to which 1 to 4 tablespoons of household ammonia has been added. Rinse and repeat treatment if necessary; launder.

IODINE — Rinse from back side of stain under cool, running water. Soak in solution of color remover, or sponge with a solution of sodium thiosulfate crystals (available at drug store). Rinse and launder.

LIPSTICK — Place face down on paper towels. Sponge area with dry-cleaning solvent, or use a prewash soil and stain remover. Replace towels frequently; rinse. Rub light-duty liquid

Tedious Tips

detergent into stain until outline is removed; launder. Repeat treatment if needed.

LIQUID PAPER — Sponge the stain with amyl acetate (banana oil). Repeat treatment if necessary. Rub gently with detergent, then launder.

MERCUROCHROME OR METHYOLATE — Rinse out as much of the stain as possible under cool, running water. Soak for 30 minutes in a solution of ½ teaspoon ammonia per quart of water. Rinse; if stain remains, soak in a solution of 1 quart warm water and 1 tablespoon vinegar for one hour. Rinse thoroughly and allow to dry. Launder with detergent and bleach. For delicate fabrics, apply alcohol and cover with pad moistened with alcohol. Change pads frequently until stain is removed. Rinse; launder.

MILDEW — Launder stained items using chlorine bleach, if safe for that fabric. Otherwise, soak in an all-fabric bleach and hot water, then launder. If some stain remains, sponge with hydrogen peroxide. Rinse and relaunder. Dry in sunlight. Badly mildewed fabrics may be damaged beyond repair.

MUD — Let dry, then brush off as much mud as possible; or rinse under running water and let soak overnight. For light stains, pretreat with a paste of detergent and water, liquid detergent, or a liquid detergent booster; launder. Pretreat heavy stains by presoaking with a laundry detergent, a product containing enzymes, or a container of water with 1/4 cup each of ammonia and liquid detergent; launder. Red clay can be rubbed with a paste of vinegar and table salt. Leave for 30 minutes. Launder with hottest water safe for that fabric and bleach. Repeat if needed.

MUSTARD — Treat with a prewash stain remover, or dampen with water and rub with bar soap. Launder with chlorine bleach, if safe for that fabric, or use an all-fabric bleach.

PAINT — Water-based paint, such as latex acrylic stains, should be rinsed in warm water while stain is still wet; launder. This stain usually cannot be removed after it dries. For oil-based paints, including varnish, use the solvent listed on the label as a thinner. If label information is unavailable, use turpentine.

Rinse. Pretreat with prewash stain remover, bar soap, or detergent. Rinse and launder.

PERFUME — Treat with prewash stain remover or liquid laundry detergent; rinse and launder.

PERSPIRATION — Treat with prewash stain remover, or dampen stain and rub with bar soap. If the color of the fabric has changed slightly, apply ammonia to fresh stain or white vinegar to old stain; rinse. Launder in hottest water safe for that fabric. Stubborn stains may respond to pretreating with a product containing enzymes, then launder using an all-fabric bleach.

PINE RESIN — Sponge the stain with cleaning fluid; let air dry. Rub with detergent and launder as usual. If stains persist, apply a few drops of household ammonia. Air dry. Launder, using liquid laundry detergent.

POLLEN *(tree or flower)* — Sponge, then flush with dry-cleaning solvent. Let air dry. Rub gently with detergent. Launder as usual, using bleach that is safe for that fabric.

RUST — Apply a commercial rust remover. Follow manufacturer's instructions. Do not use chlorine bleach on rust.

SCORCH — Launder with chlorine bleach, if safe for that fabric. Otherwise, soak in an all-fabric bleach and hot water, then launder. Note: Badly scorched stains cannot be removed.

SHOE POLISH — Pretreat liquid shoe polish with a paste of dry detergent and water; launder. Use a dull knife to scrape residue of paste shoe polish from the fabric. Pretreat with a prewash stain remover or cleaning fluid; rinse. Rub detergent into dampened area. Launder with chlorine bleach, if safe for fabric, or an all-fabric bleach.

TAR — Act quickly before stain dries. Use a dull knife to scrape excess tar from the fabric. Place stain face down on paper towels. Sponge with cleaning fluid. Replace towels frequently for better absorption. Launder, using hottest water safe for that fabric.

TOBACCO — Moisten stain and rub with bar soap; rinse. Pretreat with stain stick or soak in an enzyme solution; launder. Note: If stain remains, launder again using chlorine bleach, if safe for fabric, or use oxygen bleach.

Tedious Tips

URINE, VOMIT, MUCUS, OR FECES — Treat with prewash spray or pretreat with a product containing enzymes. Launder with chlorine bleach that is safe for fabric, or use an all-fabric bleach.

YELLOWING OF WHITE COTTONS OR LINENS — Fill washer with hot water. Add twice the detergent as normal. Place items in washer and agitate four minutes on regular cycle. Stop washer and soak clothes for 15 minutes. Restart washer and agitate 15 minutes. Complete the wash cycle. Repeat process if needed.

YELLOWING OF WHITE NYLON — Soak garment overnight in an enzyme presoak or oxygen bleach. Launder, using hot water and twice as much detergent as usual with an oxygen bleach.

General Rules

- Treat stains promptly. Fresh stains are easier to remove than old ones. If the stain is on a nonwashable fabric, take it to the dry cleaner as soon as possible. Tell the stain and the fiber content of the garment.
- Read and follow package directions when using any stain removal product.
- Always test stain removers on an inside seam or other hidden part of garment for color fastness. To test, apply product and let stand 2-5 minutes, then rinse. If color changes, do not use product on garment.
- When using a bleach, do not try to bleach just one area of garment; bleach the entire garment to prevent uneven color removal.
- When treating, place stained area face down on a clean paper towel or white cloth. Apply stain remover to the underside of the stain, forcing stain off the fabric surface instead of through it.
- Never put chemical dry-cleaning solvents directly into washer.
- Thoroughly rinse and air dry areas treated with dry-cleaning solvents before placing in washer, to avoid a fire.
- Do not mix stain removal products together. Some mixtures,

such as ammonia and chlorine bleach, can produce noxious fumes.
- Always launder washable items after treating to remove residues of the stain and the stain remover.
- Have patience; it takes a little extra time and effort to remove some stains.
- Remember, some stains cannot be removed.
- Take nonwashable items to dry cleaner as soon as possible; identify stain and fiber content of garment.

Definitions

DETERGENT — all-purpose synthetic detergent (liquid or powder). Use liquid detergent full strength; mix powder with water to form a paste when working into stain.

DRY-CLEANING SOLVENT — stain and spot removers available at grocery and hardware stores. A nonflammable type is safest to use.

Sleepercize

a. How do you get candle wax out of clothes?
b. What should you pre-treat cosmetic stains with?
c. What's the best way to remove egg stains?
d. How many parts alcohol, how many parts water should be used to get out acetate?
e. List eight examples of grease stains.
f. How do you remove lipstick?
g. Mud?
h. Mildew?

Tedious Tips

How to Get a
Good Night's Sleep

Stop working so hard trying to get to sleep—you'll tire yourself out. Here are some handy pointers to help bring on the Z's. ⓨ

> *Come, blessed barrier between day and day,*
> *Dear mother of fresh thoughts and joyous health!*
> —William Wordsworth in "To Sleep" (1806)

FOR YEARS, there were no refreshing lulls between days for Lauren Ero. Rather than waking up feeling clearheaded and healthy, the 37-year-old mother of two spent four years perpetually listless and moody.

"Those years are like a fog to me. I just remember how hard it was and how hopeless I felt," she says. "I would be more tired in the morning than when I went to bed the night before. I was too exhausted to do even day-to-day activities like taking care of my kids and things around the house."

Ero was suffering not from depression, as one doctor surmised based on her look-alike symptoms of despondent mood and irritability, but from insomnia.

The definition of insomnia, according to the American Sleep Disorders Association (ASDA), is difficulty falling asleep or staying asleep. If it occurs every night or most nights for an extended time, like Ero's, it's called chronic insomnia.

According to ASDA estimates, more than 35 million Americans suffer from this long-lasting type of insomnia, with 20 to 30 million others suffering shorter-term sleeplessness. Men and women of all ages experience insomnia, but it is more common in the elderly and in women, especially after menopause. The consequences of a "Sleepless Society" can be serious.

Overcoming Roadblocks to Sleep
Like a headache or fever, insomnia may be a symptom of another problem. It can result from something as simple as anticipating a stressful event, like a test or meeting, or from a longer-lasting stressful circumstance, such as a sick child or troubled marriage. Even worrying about having a tough time falling asleep may itself prevent a person from drifting off.

Other common causes of nighttime wakefulness include environmental disturbances, such as noise from traffic or television, an uncomfortable temperature, or light from the sun or other source; use of alcohol or stimulants, such as caffeine or nicotine; and erratic hours, like those of shift workers and people whose air travel takes them across time zones.

Sometimes short-term insomnia may go away on its own or with simple changes in daytime or sleep-time habits. (See "Wooing Sleep.") If these lifestyle changes don't work, the careful use of sleeping pills approved by the Food and Drug Administration may help provide temporary relief from insomnia. A doctor can help choose an appropriate medicine. One factor to consider is the drug's half-life, or the time it takes to be cleared from the body. Drugs with shorter half-lives are less likely to have carry-over sedation that affects daytime functioning.

A second factor is the drug's toxicity. Because of their lower risk of overdose, the newer benzodiazepines and benzodiazepine-like drugs are used more often to treat insomnia than barbiturates and other older drugs. Among the most commonly prescribed benzodiazepine sleep-aids are flurazepam (Dalmane), estazolam (ProSom), quazepam (Doral), temazepam (Restoril),

Forty Winks

and triazolam (Halcion). The prescription sleep-aid zolpidem (Ambien) is in the imidazopyridine class of drugs.

As a rule, these sleeping pills should be used only for short periods because of the risk of developing dependency and withdrawal symptoms when the drugs are stopped. So, while they may help with short-term insomnia induced by jet lag, shift work schedule changes, or short-term stress, they should generally not be used for chronic insomnia because of their potential addictiveness and because they can mask underlying medical problems.

Some other sleep-aids are available without a prescription, including diphenhydramine (in Nytol, Sleep-Eze, and Sominex) and doxylamine (in Unisom Nighttime). These products contain a sedating antihistamine and, like prescription drugs, must be used with care. Even if taken at night, they can cause daytime drowsiness, which can make driving and other tasks risky.

Sleep Apnea: More Than Simple Snoring

Unlike short-term sleeplessness, chronic insomnia is often a symptom of a serious underlying medical disorder. Depression and other psychiatric disorders account for many cases of insomnia, as do wholly physical illnesses, such as asthma, arthritis, Parkinson's disease, kidney or heart disease, and hyperthyroidism.

Sleep apnea is among the most common and most dangerous types of sleep disorder. An estimated 18 million Americans have the condition, which is marked by repeated episodes of cessation of breathing during sleep that over time can lead to high blood pressure, cardiac disease, and disordered thinking.

Sleep apnea was the culprit in Lauren Ero's case. After two years of trying various antidepressants that offered her no relief, Ero sought a second medical opinion and was sent for a sleep analysis. "Then it was really obvious what it was," says Ero, who recently began working for the American Sleep Apnea Association. "It was a classic case."

The tests revealed what Ero didn't know and what her husband hadn't found alarming: Ero was snoring. But her "snoring" problem was distinct from the merely annoying type because she was also gasping for air throughout the night—possibly tens of times each hour—which repeatedly roused her out of her refreshing, deep sleep. The results were the telltale signs of sleep apnea: excessive daytime sleepiness and difficulty functioning.

Obstructive sleep apnea is by far the most common type. Breathing is interrupted when air can't flow into or out of the nose or mouth. The reason for the blockage could be an over-relaxation of the throat muscles and tongue, which partially blocks the airway or, in obese people, an excess amount of tissue in the airway. Those with receding chin lines are also at high risk for developing obstructive sleep apnea.

In the less common form, central sleep apnea, breathing is stopped not because the airway is closed but because the diaphragm and chest muscles stop working.

Mild cases of obstructive sleep apnea can sometimes be treated by making simple behavioral changes, such as avoiding alcohol, tobacco, and sleeping pills; losing weight; and sleeping on one's side. Also, oral devices to prevent obstruction of the airway by holding the tongue or jaw forward may help with mild cases.

The most common effective treatment for obstructive sleep apnea is nasal continuous positive airway pressure, or CPAP. The patient wears a soft plastic mask over his or her nose while sleeping. A device supplies pressurized room air through a flexible tube attached to the mask. The pressurized air acts on a splint to prevent the airway from collapsing.

"You have to get used to wearing a mask while you sleep," says Ero, who has been using the CPAP device nightly since 1996. "But you feel so much better, it's worth the hassle. Within two weeks after starting to use it, I felt like a different person. I have so much energy now."

Surgery to increase the size of the airway is another possible option for sleep apnea treatment. The removal of adenoids and tonsils, especially in children, or other growths or tissue in the airway is sometimes effective, as are other, relatively more risky surgical procedures, including uvulopalatopharyngoplasty (shaving of the excess soft tissues in the mouth and throat) and tracheotomy (creating an opening in the neck through the windpipe) for the most severe cases.

The newest device for this condition is Somnoplasty, used to treat mild cases of sleep apnea. It is a radio frequency surgical device that shrinks the soft palate in a half-hour outpatient procedure. FDA approved the Somnoplasty device in July 1997.

When to Worry

Just as snoring isn't always a sign of dangerous apnea, neither is a sleepless night or two necessarily a medical emergency. Sometimes sleep patterns differ based on simple factors like age and lifestyle.

Bob Rappaport, M.D., a sleep medicine specialist, neurologist, and FDA drug reviewer, encourages people to consider getting help if their sleeplessness persists and appears to be unrelated to life circumstances.

Wooing Sleep

A jokester's definition of insomnia: When you keep a bunch of innocent sheep jumping over a fence all night just because you can't get to sleep.

Experts agree that the time-honored practice of counting sheep or doing another such monotonous task may help induce sleep. Sleep specialists provide these additional tips to help you reach dreamland.

- Avoid caffeine (including caffeine-containing drugs), nicotine, and alcohol for four to six hours before bedtime. The first two are stimulants that can make it difficult to sleep. And while alcohol may have a sedating effect at first, it tends to disturb sleep after several hours.
- Don't exercise within four to six hours of bedtime. Working out earlier in the day, though, not only doesn't hinder sleep, but can actually improve it.
- Perform relaxing rituals before bed, such as taking a warm bath, listening to relaxing music, or eating a light snack.

- Before going to bed, try as much as possible to put your worries out of your mind and plan to address them another time.
- Reserve your bed for sleeping. To preserve the association between bed and slumber, don't watch television or do work in bed.
- Go to bed only when sleepy. If you can't fall asleep within 15 to 20 minutes, get out of bed and read a book or do another relaxing activity for awhile, rather than trying harder to fall asleep.
- Make sure your bed is comfortable and the bedroom is conducive to restful sleep—quiet and at a comfortable temperature, for example.
- Wake up about the same time every day, even on weekends, to normalize the sleep-wake schedule.
- Don't take naps, or nap during the mid-afternoon for no more than 30 minutes.

Melatonin?

Many Americans in search of more satisfying slumber are buying the hormone melatonin at their local health food stores. Melatonin-containing products are marketed as dietary supplements, which can be sold without FDA's premarket review or approval.

Researchers, including those at a 1996 National Institutes of Health conference about melatonin and sleep, caution melatonin users about the absence of scientific studies to prove that melatonin is safe and helpful in treating insomnia.

"Public fervor for melatonin runs far ahead of the scientific evidence to support it," states an article about the NIH workshop in the *Journal of the American Medical Association*, referring to the reported $200 million to $350 million U.S. market for the hormone.

"People are taking melatonin and we are trying to figure out what it does," said one researcher who attended the NIH meeting. "We are going about it backward."

NIH sleep expert James Kiley, M.D., agrees that many questions about the supplement remain unanswered: "We need some research to address the concerns about melatonin and its safety and efficacy."

Sleepercize

List the long term effect of sleep deprivation. Re-read this passage. How many of these effects are you experiencing—NO! Forget it—that's the last thing you should be worrying about right now.

Dietary Fiber

As long as you're up, you may as well worry about getting enough fiber. Here's more than you probably ever wanted to know on this burning issue. Hint: one page of this book, eaten dry, supplies 300% of your daily recommended intake of wood pulp. Ⓨ

A "good" source of fiber contains 3 grams to less than 5 grams. A "high" source of fiber contains 5 grams or more.

BEANS & PEAS:	AMOUNT	FIBER (GRAMS)
Baked Beans, canned	½ cup	5-10
Black Beans, cooked	½ cup	4
Garbanzo, cooked	½ cup	5
Great Northern, cooked	½ cup	5
Lentils, cooked	½ cup	5
Navy (Pea) Beans, cooked	½ cup	5
Sweet Beans (Soybeans), cooked	1 cup	6-8

BREADS & CRACKERS:	AMOUNT	FIBER (GRAMS)
Pumpernickel	1 oval slice	2
Whole Wheat	1 slice	2
RyKrisp	2 crackers	4
Triscuit (Whole Wheat Wafer)	7 wafers	4

CEREALS:	AMOUNT	FIBER (GRAMS)
All-Bran	½ cup	10-16
Bran Buds	½ cup	12
Bran Flakes	½ cup	3-5
Granola	½ cup	4
Grape Nuts	½ cup	7
Oat Bran, cooked	½ cup	6
Oatmeal, cooked	½ cup	3
Raisin Bran	1 cup	5-7
Shredded Wheat	2 biscuits—1 cup	4-5
Wheat Bran	1 ¼–1 ½ cups	2-10
Wheat Germ	¼ cup	2-4
Whole Wheat Wheaties	1 cup	3

FRUITS:	AMOUNT	FIBER (GRAMS)
Apple, with skin	1 medium	3
Apricot, dried	10 halves	3
Avocado	⅓ medium	2
Banana	1 medium	2
Cantaloupe	¼ medium	2
Dates, dried	5	2
Figs, dried	3	5
Grapefruit	½ medium	2
Grapes, red or green	1 ½ cups	3
Kiwi	2 medium	5
Orange	1 medium	3
Pear, fresh	1 medium	5
Pineapple, fresh	1 cup	2
Plums, fresh	2 small	2
Prunes, dried	3	3
Raisins, uncooked	½ cup	3
Raspberries, fresh	1 cup	6
Strawberries, fresh	1 cup	3
Tangerine	2 medium	3

Grains/Rice/Pasta	Amount	Fiber (Grams)
Barley, cooked	½ cup	4
Bulgar, cooked	½ cup	4
Couscous, cooked	½ cup	4
Brown or Wild Rice, cooked	1 cup	3
Whole Wheat Pasta, cooked	1 cup	4

Vegetables	Amount	Fiber (Grams)
Asparagus, cooked	5 spears	2
Beans, green, cooked	1 cup	2
Beets, cooked	½ cup	2
Bell Pepper, raw	½ cup	2
Broccoli, cooked	½ cup	3
Brussels Sprouts, cooked	½ cup	3
Cabbage, green, cooked	½ cup	2
Carrot, raw	1 medium	2
Cauliflower, raw	1 cup	3
Celery, raw	3 stalks	3
Corn, cooked	1 cup	3
Green Peas, cooked	½ cup	3
Lima Beans, cooked	½ cup	6
Potato, baked with skin	1 medium	3
Spinach, raw	1 cup	2
Squash, winter, cooked	½ cup	3
Sweet Potato, baked with skin	1 medium	4
Tomato, raw	1 medium	2

Sleepercize

Remember every meal you've eaten for the past four days. In detail. Next, figure out which of these foods have dietary fiber. List each in your head, then go back to the chart and count your dietary fiber quotient for the past four days.

Your Boring Body

Sea Turtles

As you lie in your bedroom wide awake, imagine all the transmitter-fitted sea turtles migrating placidly through silent seas. Or better yet, read this piece about the tagging project and imagine how tiring it must have been. ✆

AUGUST 13, 1999—NOAA announced today that a satellite tagging project that gives biologists a rare opportunity to study one of the nation's most amazing and endangered marine animals— loggerhead sea turtles—is being carried out by NOAA Fisheries and the U.S. Fish and Wildlife Service, in partnership with the Florida Fish and Wildlife Conservation Commission and the Caribbean Conservation Corporation.

"We expect this project to provide the agencies with valuable information for making management decisions that will help to ensure the survival of this species," said Barbara Schroeder, the national sea turtle coordinator with NOAA Fisheries and a member of the research tagging team. "Up until very recently, studies of sea turtles were conducted primarily while the turtles nested on ocean beaches—an activity that accounts for less than 1 percent of their life span. Now, we are able to peer into the interesting and critical behavioral aspects of their life cycles away from their nesting beaches, which will have a great bearing on the recovery of this species and, ultimately, their survival."

The collaborative effort is utilizing satellite transmitters attached to the turtle's shell to identify migratory pathways and destinations of Florida loggerheads after they nest. The collected data will help scientists address the threats that sea turtles may encounter while traveling to and from their nesting beaches. The information will contribute to larger efforts helping to ensure the survival of the species.

The work will be conducted along the east and west coasts of Florida, including the Archie Carr National Wildlife Refuge centered at Melbourne Beach, Florida. Florida beaches account for 90 percent of the nesting of loggerheads in the southeast U.S., a population that is the largest in the western hemisphere and one of the two largest in the world. The loggerhead was listed in 1978 as a threatened species under the Endangered Species Act.

"Understanding migratory routes and principal foraging habitats of U.S. nesting loggerheads will allow us to determine what threats exist and what measures are needed to protect the turtles and their habitats away from the nesting beach," said Sandy MacPherson, National Sea Turtle Coordinator of the U.S. Fish and Wildlife Service and a member of the tagging team. "This information is vitally important to determine where international cooperative efforts are needed to ensure recovery of our shared sea turtle resources."

The public can participate in the loggerhead's journey electronically as part of a public education project spearheaded by the Gainesville based non-profit Caribbean Conservation Corporation's Sea Turtle Survival League. The travels of some of the turtles that will be tagged this summer will be posted at the CCC's Web site at www.cccturtle.org.

"Through the Sea Turtle Survival League's education program, thousands of people around the U.S. and the world, especially school children, can follow the migrations of sea turtles and learn about them, the threats they face, and how to take part in helping to ensure their survival," said Dan Evans, Sea Turtle Survival League Education Coordinator.

The Stultifying Natural World

The tagging team will attach satellite transmitters to adult female turtles that have just finished nesting. Each transmitter is a rectangular box about the size of a small, handheld radio. It is attached to the shell with fiberglass cloth and resin and is designed to fall off harmlessly when the batteries are no longer operational. The transmitter sends out radio signals through a small antenna to be picked up by one of several polar orbiting NOAA satellites that collect environmental data around the world. The satellite re-transmits the data to earth where it is processed and made available to the researcher in a usable format. Movements are monitored "remotely" and the researcher is not required to be in close proximity to the turtle. Depending on a number of factors, including the length of time the turtle is at the surface and the position of the satellites relative to the turtle, the location of the turtle can be calculated to within 150 meters of its actual position.

"This great advance in technology allows us to really go where no one has gone before—on a long-distance migration with a sea turtle," commented Dr. Allen Foley, an Assistant Research Scientist with the Florida Fish and Wildlife Conservation Commission's Florida Marine Research Institute and a member of the tagging team. "With satellite telemetry, we essentially receive one or more e-mails a week from each of our turtles reporting their current positions."

Scientists with NOAA Fisheries and the Florida Marine Research Institute implemented a preliminary study in 1998 and, using satellite telemetry technology, are learning much about the migratory movements and places of residence of loggerhead turtles that nest in Florida. Results from 1998 indicate that the post-nesting loggerheads cover large distances and some travel through and reside in the waters of nations other than the U.S., including Cuba, the Bahamas, and Mexico.

Loggerheads are reddish-brown in color with yellow-bordered scales on the top and sides of the head and top of the flippers. The neck, shoulders, and limb bases are usually dull brown on top and medium yellow on the sides and bottom. The average size of an adult loggerhead is about 36 inches (92 cm) and they usually weigh about 250 lbs. (115 kg). The average size at hatching is a little under 2 inches long, a size that can fit in the palm of your hand. Maturity is reached at between 16-40 years. Mating takes place in late March-early June, and eggs are laid throughout the summer.

Loggerheads remain threatened by accidental capture in trawl, net, and longline fisheries and their habitat, which is critical to their survival, is threatened and destroyed by coastal development, especially beachfront armoring and artificial lighting, increased human use of nesting beaches, and marine pollution. Loggerheads inhabit the continental shelf, bays, estuaries, and lagoons in temperate, subtropical, and tropical waters. In the Atlantic, the loggerhead range extends from Newfoundland to as far south as Argentina. The primary Atlantic nesting sites are along the east coast of Florida, with additional sites in Georgia, the Carolinas, and the Gulf Coast of Florida

Soporific Classics

Genesis 36:15

For long repetitive stretches, you just can't beat the Bible. Here's a choice genealogy of the descendents of Esau (brother of Jacob) to dull your senses. ⓨ

15: THESE WERE THE CHIEFS among Esau's descendants:

The sons of Eliphaz the firstborn of Esau: Chiefs Teman, Omar, Zepho, Kenaz, Korah, Gatam and Amalek.

16: These were the chiefs descended from Eliphaz in Edom; they were grandsons of Adah.

17: The sons of Esau's son Reuel: Chiefs Nahath, Zerah, Shammah and Mizzah. These were the chiefs descended from Reuel in Edom; they were grandsons of Esau's wife Basemath.

18: The sons of Esau's wife Oholibamah: Chiefs Jeush, Jalam and Korah. These were the chiefs descended from Esau's wife Oholibamah daughter of Anah.

19: These were the sons of Esau (that is, Edom), and these were their chiefs.

20: These were the sons of Seir the Horite, who were living in the region: Lotan, Shobal, Zibeon, Anah,

21: Dishon, Ezer and Dishan. These sons of Seir in Edom were Horite chiefs.

22: The sons of Lotan: Hori and Homan. Timna was Lotan's sister.

23: The sons of Shobal: Alvan, Manahath, Ebal, Shepho and Onam.

24: The sons of Zibeon: Aiah and Anah. This is the Anah who discovered the hot springs in the desert while he was grazing the donkeys of his father Zibeon.

25: The children of Anah: Dishon and Oholibamah daughter of Anah.

26: The sons of Dishon: Hemdan, Eshban, Ithran and Keran.

27: The sons of Ezer: Bilban, Zaavan and Akan.

28: The sons of Dishan: Uz and Aran.

29: These were the Horite chiefs: Lotan, Shobal, Zibeon, Anah, Dishon, Ezer and Dishan.

30: These were the Horite chiefs according to their divisions, in the land of Seir.

The Rulers of Edom

31: These were the kings who reigned in Edom before any Israelite king reigned:

32: Bela son of Beor became kind of Edom. His city was named Dinhabah.

33: When Bela died, Jobab son of Zerah from Bozrah succeeded him as king.

34: When Jobab died, Husham from the land of the Temanites succeeded him as king.

35: When Husham died, Hadad son of Bedad, who defeated Midian in the country of Moab, succeeded him as king. His city was named Avith.

36: When Hadad died, Samlah from Masrekah succeeded him as king.

37: When Samlah died, Shaul from Rehoboth on the river succeeded him as king.

38: When Shaul died, Baal-Hanan son of Achor succeeded him as king.

Sleepercize

In your mind, trace your lineage as far back as you can. Picture it as a "family tree"—do not get out of bed and draw it.

President Clinton's Grand Jury Testimony

Bill Clinton may fret over his legacy, but we can say with assurance that the 42nd president proved overwhelmingly that sex—or at least talking about it—is a big snooze. Of course, that depends on what your definition of "snooze" is. ⚉

WASHINGTON (AP)—Text of President Clinton's Aug. 17 grand jury testimony before Office of the Independent Counsel prosecutors investigating the president's relationship with former White House intern Monica Lewinsky. The following transcripts were provided by the Federal Document Clearing House:

(Unknown)	Mr. President, would you raise your right hand please? Do you solemnly swear that the testimony you're about to give in this matter will be the truth, the whole truth, and nothing but the truth, so help you God?
Clinton	I do.
Question	Good afternoon, Mr. President.
Clinton	Good afternoon.
Question	Could you please state your full name for the record, sir?
Clinton	William Jefferson Clinton.
Question	My name is Sol Wisenberg. I'm a deputy inde-

	pendent counsel with the Office of Independent Counsel. And with me today are some other attorneys from the Office of Independent Counsel. At the courthouse are the ladies and gentlemen of the grand jury prepared to receive your testimony as you give it. Do you understand, sir?
Clinton	Yes, I do.
Question	This proceeding is subject to Rule 6(e) of the federal rules of criminal procedure as modified by Judge Johnson's order. You are appearing voluntarily today as part of an agreement worked out between your attorney, the Office of the Independent Counsel, and with the approval of Judge Johnson. Is that correct, sir?
Clinton	This is correct.
(Unknown)	Mr. Wisenberg, excuse me. You referred to Judge Johnson's order. I'm not familiar with that order. Have we been served that or not?
Question	No. My understanding is that that is an order that the judge is going to sign today. She didn't have the name of Awaka (ph). A person—basically, my understanding is that it will cover all of the attorneys here today and the technical people in the room. So that they would be authorized personally to be permitted to hear grand jury testimony that they otherwise wouldn't be authorized to hear.
(Unknown)	Thank you.
Question	The grand jury, Mr. President, has been empaneled by a United States District Court for the District of Columbia. Do you understand that, sir?
Clinton	I do.
Question	And among other things, it's currently investigating under the authority of the Court of Appeals upon application by the attorney general whether Monica Lewinsky or others obstructed justice, intimidated witnesses, or committed other crimes

	related to the case of *Jones v. Clinton.* Do you understand that, sir?
Clinton	I do.
Question	And today, you will be receiving questions not only from attorneys on the OIC staff, but from some of the grand jurors, too. Do you understand that?
Clinton	Yes, sir. I do.
Question	I'm going to talk briefly about your rights and responsibilities as a grand jury witness. Normally, grand jury witnesses, while not allowed to have attorneys in the grand jury room, can stop and consult with their attorneys. But our arrangement today, your attorneys are here and present for consultation *(off-mike)* to consult with them as necessary, but it won't count against *(off-mike)*. Do you understand that, sir?
Clinton	I do understand that.
Question	You have a privilege against self-incrimination. If a truthful answer to any question would tend to incriminate you, you can invoke the privilege and that application will not be used against you. Do you understand that?
Clinton	I do.
Question	And if you don't invoke it, however, any of the answers that you do give can and will be used against you. Do you understand that, sir?
Clinton	I do.
Question	And do you understand that because you've been sworn to tell the truth, the whole truth, and nothing but the truth, that if you were to lie or intentionally mislead the grand jury you could be prosecuted for perjury and/or obstruction of justice?
Clinton	I believe that's correct.
Question	Is there anything that you—I have stated to you regarding your rights and responsibilities that you

	would like me to clarify that you don't understand?
Clinton	No, sir.
Question	Mr. President, I'd like to read for you a portion of federal ... (ph) 603, which discusses the important function the oath has in our judicial system. It says that the purpose of the oath is 1) quote, "calculated to awaken the witness' conscience and impress the witness' mind with the duty," end quote—to tell the truth. Could you please tell the grand jury what that oath means to you for today's testimony?
Clinton	I have sworn an oath to tell the truth and that's what I intend to do.
Question	You understand it requires you to give the whole truth, that is a complete answer to each question, sir?
Clinton	I will answer each question as accurately and fully as I can.
Question	Now, you took the same oath to tell the truth, the whole truth, and nothing but the truth on January 17, 1998, in a deposition in the Paul Jones litigation, is that correct, sir?
Clinton	I did take an oath there.
Question	Did the oath you took on that occasion mean the same to you then as it does today?
Clinton	I believed then that I had to answer the questions truthfully, that's correct.
Question	I'm sorry, I didn't hear you, sir.
Clinton	I believe that I had to answer the questions truthfully, that's correct.
Question	And it meant the same to you then as it does today?
Clinton	Well, no one read me a definition then and we didn't go through this exercise then. I swore an oath to tell the truth and I believed I was bound to be truthful and I tried to be.

Question	At the Paula Jones deposition, you were represented by Mr. Robert Bennett, your counsel, is that correct?
Clinton	That is correct.
Question	He was authorized by you to be your representative, or your attorney, is that correct?
Clinton	That is correct.
Question	Your counsel, Mr. Bennett, indicated that—page five of the deposition, lines 10 to 12, I'm quoting: "The president intends to give full and complete answers as Ms. Jones is entitled to have." End of quote.
Question	My question to you is—Do you agree with your counsel that his client in the sexual harassment case is, to use his words, "entitled to have the truth"?
Clinton	I believe that I was bound to give truthful answers. Yes, sir.
Question	But the question is, sir, do you agree with your counsel that a plaintiff in a sexual harassment case is entitled to have the truth?
Clinton	I believe when a witness is under oath in a civil case or otherwise under oath, the witness should do everything possible to answer the questions truthfully.
Question	I want to turn over questioning now to Mr. Bittman of our office, Mr. President.
Question	Good afternoon, Mr. President.
Clinton	Good afternoon, Mr. Bittman.
Question	My name is Robert Bittman. I'm an attorney with the Office of Independent Counsel. Mr. President, we are first going to turn to some of the details of your relationship with Monica Lewinsky that follow on your deposition that you provided in the Paula Jones case as was referenced on January 17, 1998. The questions are uncomfortable and I apologize for that in advance. I'll try to

	be as brief and direct as possible. Mr. President, were you physically intimate with Monica Lewinsky?
Clinton	Mr. Bittman, I think maybe I can save the—you and the grand jurors a lot of time if I read a statement which I think will make it clear what the nature of my relationship with Ms. Lewinsky was, how it related to the testimony I gave, what I was trying to do in that testimony. And I think it will perhaps make it possible for you to ask even more relevant questions from your point of view.
Clinton	And with your permission, I'd like to read that statement.
Unknown	Absolutely. Please, Mr. President.
Clinton	When I was alone with Ms. Lewinsky on certain occasions in early 1996, and once in early 1997, I engaged in conduct that was wrong. These encounters did not consist of sexual intercourse. They did not constitute sexual relations, as I understood that term to be defined at my January 17th, 1998, deposition. But they did involve inappropriate, intimate contact. These inappropriate encounters ended at my insistence in early 1997. I also had occasional telephone conversations with Ms. Lewinsky that included inappropriate sexual banter. I regret that what began as a friendship came to include this conduct. And I take full responsibility for my actions. While I will provide the grand jury whatever other information I can, because of privacy considerations affecting my family, myself, and others, and in an effort to preserve the dignity of the office I hold, this is all I will say about the specifics of these particular matters. I will try to answer to the best of my ability other questions, including questions about my relationship with Ms. Lewinsky, questions about my understanding of the

term of sexual relations, as I understood it to be defined at my January 17, 1998, deposition, and questions concerning alleged subornation of perjury, obstruction of justice, and intimidation of witnesses.

Clinton That, Mr. Bittman, is my statement.

Question Thank you, Mr. President. And we would like to take a break.

Clinton Would you like to have this?

Question Yes, please. As a matter of fact, why don't we have that marked as grand jury exhibit WBAC-1 (ph).

Clinton So, are we going to take a break?

Question Yes, we'll take a break. And we have the camera off now, please.

Question Mr. President, your statement indicates that your contacts with Ms. Lewinsky did not involve any inappropriate intimate contact. Mr. Bittman . . .

Clinton No, sir, it indicates that it did involve inappropriate intimate contact.

Question Okay, it did involve inappropriate intimate contact.

Clinton Yes, sir, it did.

(Unknown) Mr. Bittman, the witness does not have a copy of his statement. We just have the one copy.

Question *(off-mike)*

(Unknown) Thank you.

Question Was this contact with Ms. Lewinksy—Mr. President, did it involve any sexual contact in any way, shape, or form?

Clinton Mr. Bittmann, I said in this statement I would like to stay to the terms of the statement. I think it's clear what inappropriately intimate is. I have said what it did not include. It did not include sexual intercourse, and I did not believe that it included conduct which falls within the definition I was given in the Jones deposition. And I would like to stay with that characterization.

Question	*(off-mike)* rule 2, the definition that was provided you during your deposition. We'll have that marked as grand jury exhibit WJC2. This is an exact copy, Mr. President, of the exhibit that was provided you during that deposition. And I'm sure you remember throughout the deposition, that paragraph 1 of the deposition remained in effect, that Judge Wright ruled that that was to be the guiding definition in that paragraphs 2 and 3 were stricken. Do you remember that, Mr. President?
Clinton	Yes. Specifically what I remembered is there were two different discussions, I think, of this. There was quite an extended one in the beginning. And everybody was entering into it. And then in the end, the judge said that she would take the—excuse me—the first definition and strike the rest of it. That's my memory.
Question	Did you—well, at page 19 of your deposition in the case the attorney who provided you with the deposition asked you—Would you please take whatever time you need to read the deposition.
Question	And later on in the deposition, you did, of course, refer to the deposition several times. Were you, during the deposition, familiar with the definition?
Clinton	Yes, sir. My—let me just ask a question. If you're going to ask me about my deposition, could I have a copy of it? Does anybody have a copy of it?
Question	We have a copy we'll provide your counsel.
Question	*(off-mike)* entered into the *(off-mike)*
Clinton	Now, you say that was on page 19, Mr. Bittman?
Question	Page 19, Mr. President, beginning at line 21. I will read in it full. This is from the Jones attorney. "Would you please take whatever time you need

for this definition because when I use the term sexual relations, this is what I mean today."

Clinton   Yes, sir. That stops on 19. Let me say that there is—just for the record—if my recollection is accurate—there was a long discussion here between the attorneys and the judge. It goes on until page 23, and in the end, the judge said, I'm talking about only about part one in the definition. And do you understand that? And I answered, "I do." So the judge says part one and then the lawyer for Ms. Jones says he's only talking about part one. And they asked me if I understand it, and I say I do. And that was my understanding. I might also note that when I was given this and began to ask questions about it, I circled number one. This is my circle here. I remember doing that so I could focus only on those two lines, which is what I did.

Question   Did you understand the word in the first portion of the exhibit, Mr. President? That is for the purposes of this definition, the person who engages in—quote, unquote—"sexual relations" that a person knowingly engages in or causes—did you understand—do you understand the words there in that phrase?

Clinton   Yes. My—I can tell you what my understanding of the definition is.

Question   Sure.

Clinton   If you want me to, let's (ph) do it. My understanding of this definition is that it covers contact by the person being deposed with the enumerated areas, if the contact is done with an intent to arouse or gratify. That's my understanding of the definition.

Question   What did you believe the definition to include and exclude? What kind of exclusions?

Clinton   I thought the definition included any activity by the person being deposed where the person was the actor and came in contact with those parts of the body with the purpose or intent of gratification, and excluded any other activity. For example, kissing's not covered by that, I don't think.

Question Did you understand the definition to be limited to sexual activity?

Clinton Yes, I understood the definition to be limited to physical contact with those areas of the body with the specific intent to arouse or gratify. That's what I understood it to be.

Question What specific acts did the definition include, as you understood the definition on January 17th, 1998?

Clinton Any contact with the areas that are mentioned, sir. If you contacted those parts of the body with an intent to arouse or gratify, that is covered.

Question What did you understand . . .

Clinton The person being deposed. If the person being deposed contacted those parts of another person's body with an intent to arouse or gratify, that was covered.

Question What did you understand the word "causes" in the first phrase to mean? For the purposes of this deposition, the person engages in sexual relations when the person knowingly causes contact?

Clinton I don't know what that means. I doesn't make any sense to me in this context, because I think what I thought was since this was some sort of, as I remember they said in the previous discussion— and I'm only remembering now, so if I make a mistake, you can correct me—is I remember from the previous discussion they said this was some kind of definition that had something to do with sexual harassment. So, that implies as forcing to me. And there was never any issue of forcing in the case involving—well, any of these questions they were asking me. They made it clear in this discussion I just reviewed that what they were referring to was intentional sexual conduct, not some sort of forcible abusive behavior.

Sleepercize

How many times in this passage does President Clinton use the phrase "Yes sir?"

Moonlighting

Did you know that a quarter of all Americans work at night jobs? As you lie there in your bed tossing and turning, imagine for a moment that you have to get up and go to work. If that doesn't send you into a sound sleep, nothing will. ✪

YOU MIGHT BE SURPRISED to know that over 25 percent of all American adults hold night jobs, either to supplement their income or full-time, because they are naturally night owls or prefer their time off during waking hours. Some of the most typical night jobs include:

1. Doctors, nurses, and other hospital employees
2. Bakers
3. Road construction crews
4. Air traffic controllers
5. Writers
6. Janitors and other maintenance professionals
7. Taxi drivers
8. Long-distance truck drivers
9. Kinko employees
10. Astronomers
11. Morticians

12. Crisis line workers
13. Computer hackers
14. Obstetricians
15. Telephone operators
16. Firefighters
17. Hotel clerks
18. Zoo keepers
19. New mothers
20. Drug dealers
21. Pizza delivery people (in large cities)
22. Car impound lot employees
23. The police force

Sleepercize

Add ten more jobs to the list that can be done at night when other people—unlike you—are sleeping.

Deathly Documents

Tedious Tips

Taming the Paper Trail

You can't sleep. Is it because of the piles of paper littering your office and your home? These facts won't clear up the clutter, but at least you'll have something to blame it on. See if that doesn't put your tormented mind to rest. Ⓨ

WHETHER YOU MANAGE an office at home or at a big company, organizing and tracking important papers can be one of the top ways to improve your bottom line. Despite early predictions, modern technology means more—not less—paper to handle in business and personal matters.

There are at least five reasons papers pile up on so many desks, according to the experts:

1. Computer printers. Office copiers and laser printers turned out an estimated 1.6 trillion sheets of paper in 1996 and the number is expected to grow to 2.3 trillion sheets by 2001. Perhaps as a result of the increase in paper use, shredder use is also up.

"We have seen the paper shredder category sales increase 20 percent from 1994 to 1997," commented Tony Storrie, vice president and general manager of Business Machines at Fellowes Manufacturing, a global leader in quality organizational products for home and office. "We feel this interest and increase is due to personal privacy concerns and the enormous amounts of printed information generated by computers."

2. Computer crashes. Fear of crashing encourages printing and filing hard copies of important documents. The *Wall Street Journal* reports 95 percent of all records are stored on paper.

3. Downloading and e-mail. The enormous amount of information accessible over the Internet has changed the way we collect data. We collect and download books, maps, and news. Rather than read each item on a computer screen, people print it all out to read later or file for the future.

Meanwhile, e-mails are often printed out so recipients know they're following instructions properly. Estimates Storrie, "E-mail has increased paper printing by 40 percent."

4. Memos, spreadsheets, and desktop publishing. Software programs can easily detail corporate financial information, but it's difficult to read all the information on the screen. Printed reports are generally considered easier to read, review, and circulate.

According to *Growth Strategies,* a business newsletter, paper consumption has increased at a rate of eight percent a year since the mid-eighties, partly because desktop publishing means many people can create their own newsletters, brochures, and holiday greetings.

5. Signatures. Few managers accept a typewritten signature or initial on a contract. It's simply professional courtesy to sign letters and memos. Signed contracts and memos are then filed away.

Bearing these facts in mind may help you come to terms with your own paper chase.

Tedious Tips

The Declaration of Independence

Admit it: you know the document by sight, but when have you ever read the Declaration of Independence? Go on, give it a read-through. You think you're tired now? Just you wait. Ⓨ

IN CONGRESS, July 4, 1776

The unanimous Declaration of the thirteen united States of America,

When, in the course of human events, it becomes necessary for one people to dissolve the political bonds which have connected them with another, and to assume among the powers of the earth, the separate and equal station to which the laws of nature and of nature's God entitle them, a decent respect to the opinions of mankind requires that they should declare the causes which impel them to the separation. We hold these truths to be self-evident, that all men are created equal, that they are endowed by their Creator with certain unalienable rights, that among these are life, liberty and the pursuit of happiness. That to secure these rights, governments are instituted among men, deriving their just powers form the consent of the governed. That whenever any form of government becomes destructive to these ends, it is the right of the people to alter or to abolish it, and to institute new government, laying its foundation on such principles and organizing its powers in such form, as to them shall seem most likely to effect their safety and happiness. Prudence, indeed, will dictate that governments long established should not be changed for light and transient causes; and accordingly all experience hath shown that mankind are more disposed to suffer, while evils are sufferable, than to right themselves by abolishing the forms to which they are accustomed. But when a long train of abuses and usurpations, pursuing invariably the same object evinces a design to reduce them under absolute despotism, it is their right, it is their duty, to throw off such government, and to provide new guards for their future security. —Such has been the patient sufferance of these colonies; and such is now the necessity which constrains them to alter their former systems of government. The history of the present King of Great Britain is a history of repeated injuries and usurpations, all having in direct object the establishment of an absolute tyranny over these states. To prove this, let facts be submitted to a candid world. He has refused his assent to laws, the most wholesome and necessary for the public good. He has forbidden his governors to pass laws of immediate and pressing importance, unless suspended in their operation till his assent should be obtained; and when so suspended, he has utterly neglected to attend to them. He has refused to pass other laws for the accommodation of large districts of people, unless those people would relinquish the right of representation in the legislature, a right inestimable to them and formidable to tyrants only. He has called together legislative bodies at places unusual, uncomfortable, and distant from the depository of their public records, for the sole purpose of fatiguing them into compliance with his measures. He has dissolved representative houses repeatedly, for opposing with manly firmness his invasions on the rights of the people. He has refused for a long time, after such dissolutions, to cause others to be elected; whereby the legislative powers, incapable of annihilation, have returned to the people at large for their exercise; the state remaining in the meantime exposed to all the dangers of invasion from without, and convulsions within. He has endeavored to prevent the population of these states; for that purpose obstructing the

Great (Dull) Moments in History

laws for naturalization of foreigners; refusing to pass others to encourage their migration hither, and raising the conditions of new appropriations of lands. He has obstructed the administration of justice, by refusing his assent to laws for establishing judiciary powers. He has made judges dependent on his will alone, for the tenure of their offices, and the amount and payment of their salaries. He has erected a multitude of new offices, and sent hither swarms of officers to harass our people, and eat out their substance. He has kept among us, in times of peace, standing armies without the consent of our legislature. He has affected to render the military independent of and superior to civil power. He has combined with others to subject us to a jurisdiction foreign to our constitution, and unacknowledged by our laws; giving his assent to their acts of pretended legislation: For quartering large bodies of armed troops among us: For protecting them, by mock trial, from punishment for any murders which they should commit on the inhabitants of these states: For cutting off our trade with all parts of the world: For imposing taxes on us without our consent: For depriving us in many cases, of the benefits of trial by jury: For transporting us beyond seas to be tried for pretended offenses: For abolishing the free system of English laws in a neighboring province, establishing therein an arbitrary government, and enlarging its boundaries so as to render it at once an example and fit instrument for introducing the same absolute rule in these colonies: For taking away our charters, abolishing our most valuable laws, and altering fundamentally the forms of our governments: For suspending our own legislatures, and declaring themselves invested with power to legislate for us in all cases whatsoever. He has abdicated government here, by declaring us out of his protection and waging war against us. He has plundered our seas, ravaged our coasts, burned our towns, and destroyed the lives of our people. He is at this time transporting large armies of foreign mercenaries to complete the works of death, desolation and tyranny, already begun with circumstances of cruelty and perfidy scarcely paralleled in the most barbarous ages, and totally unworthy the head of a civilized nation. He has constrained our fellow citizens taken captive on the high seas to bear arms against their country, to become the executioners of their friends and brethren, or to fall themselves by their hands. He has excited domestic insurrections amongst us, and has endeavored to bring on the inhabitants of our frontiers, the merciless Indian savages, whose known rule of warfare, is undistinguished destruction of all ages, sexes and conditions. In every stage of these oppressions we have petitioned for redress in the most humble terms: our repeated petitions have been answered only by repeated injury. A prince, whose character is thus marked by every act which may define a tyrant, is unfit to be the ruler of a free people. Nor have we been wanting in attention to our British brethren. We have warned them from time to time of attempts by their legislature to extend an unwarrantable jurisdiction over us. We have reminded them of the circumstances of our emigration and settlement here. We have appealed to their native justice and magnanimity, and we have conjured them by the ties of our common kindred to disavow these usurpations, which would inevitably interrupt our connections and correspondence. We must, therefore, acquiesce in the necessity, which denounces our separation, and hold them, as we hold the rest of mankind, enemies in war, in peace friends. We, therefore, the representatives of the United States of America, in General Congress, assembled, appealing to the Supreme Judge of the world for the rectitude of our intentions, do, in the name, and by the authority of the good people of these colonies, solemnly publish and declare, that these united colonies are, and of right ought to be free and independent states; that they are absolved from all allegiance to the British Crown, and that all political connection between them and the state of Great Britain, is and ought to be totally dissolved; and that as free and independent states, they have full power to levy war, conclude peace, contract alliances, establish commerce, and to do all other acts and things which independent states may of right do. And for the support of this declaration, with a firm reliance on the protection of Divine Providence, we mutually pledge to each other our lives, our fortunes and our sacred honor.

John Hancock   Benj. Harrison   Lewis Morris

Great (Dull) Moments in History

Button Gwinnett	Thos. Nelson, Jr.	Richd. Stockton
Lyman Hall	Francis Lightfoot Lee	Jno. Witherspoon
Geo. Walton	Carter Braxton	Fras. Hopkinson
Wm. Hooper	Robt. Morris	John Hart
Joseph Hewes	Benjamin Rush	Abra. Clark
John Penn	Benj. Franklin	Josiah Bartlett
Edward Rutledge	John Morton	Wm. Whipple
Thos. Heyward, Jr.	Geo. Clymer	Saml. Adams
Thomas Lynch, Jr.	Jas. Smith	John Adams
Arthur Middleton	Geo. Taylor	Robt. Treat Paine
Samuel Chase	James Wilson	Elbridge Gerry
Wm. Paca	Geo. Ross	Step. Hopkins
Thos. Stone	Caesar Rodney	William Ellery
Charles Carroll	Geo. Read	Roger Sherman
of Carrollton	Tho. McKean	Sam. Huntington
George Wythe	Wm. Floyd	Wm. Williams
Richard Henry Lee	Phil. Livingston	Oliver Wolcott
Th. Jefferson	Frans. Lewis	Matthew Thornton

Sleepercize

List the fifty states in alphabetical order.
Now list the states backward in alphabetical order.

Hair Loss

*Tiresome words on a tiresome subject, especially if it doesn't afflict
you. Read and empathize, if you can keep your eyes open.* Ⓨ

BECAUSE OF ITS IMPORTANCE, anything that happens to our
hair that we can't control—falling out or turning gray, for
instance—can be the source of much anxiety.

In the United States, some 35 million men are losing or have
lost their hair from male-pattern baldness, according to the
American Hair Loss Council. Approximately 20 million women
have experienced a similar loss of hair (from female-pattern hair
loss), and an estimated 2.5 million Americans have lost their hair
due to other causes.

The Basics

Hair is produced by hair follicles—indentations of the epidermis
(outer skin layer) that contain the hair root, the muscle attached
to it, and sebaceous, or oil, glands. Hair is made up of dead cells
filled with proteins, most of which are known as keratins. The
cells are woven together like a rope to form the hair fiber. The
hair fiber, in turn, has three layers: the outer cuticle with its fish-
scale-like structure; the cortex, which contains the bulk of the

fiber; and the center, or medulla. Hair color is determined by melanocytes, cells that produce pigment. When these cells stop producing pigment, hair turns gray.

Although it seems as if the hair on your head is always growing, hair actually has active and rest phases. The growth phase, known as anagen, lasts for two to six years. At any given time, about 90 percent of scalp hair is in the growth stage. The remainder is in the rest phase, known as telogen; this lasts from two to three months.

Once the rest phase is over, the hair strand falls out and a new one begins to grow. As a result, it's considered normal to lose from 20 to 100 hairs a day, says Diana Bihova, M.D., a dermatologist in private practice in New York City. Only a change in your regular pattern of loss is considered abnormal—but many things, including genetic factors, diet, stress, and medications, can change that pattern.

Baldness: Manifest Destiny?

The most common cause of hair loss in both men and women is rooted in a genetic predisposition. Called androgenic alopecia, it is known as male-pattern baldness in men and female-pattern hair loss in women (alopecia is the scientific term for baldness). According to the American Hair Loss Council, genetics accounts for 95 percent of all cases of hair loss in this country.

Baldness results from a combination of genetic factors and levels of testosterone (a hormone produced by the adrenal gland in both sexes and also by the testes in men). If hormone levels are right, then the hair follicles will express their genetic destiny by growing for shorter periods and producing finer hairs. In men, who have higher levels of testosterone than women, this eventually results in a bald scalp at the crown of the head and a horseshoe-shaped fringe of hair remaining on the sides. In women, the hair thins all over the scalp; the hairline does not recede. This type of hair loss doesn't usually show up in women until menopause; until then, estrogen tends to counteract the effects of testosterone.

One Approved Drug

The only drug approved by the Food and Drug Administration to treat pattern baldness or hair loss is minoxidil topical solution (Rogaine), which is rubbed into the scalp. Originally approved for hereditary male-pattern baldness in 1988, it was also approved for treating female-pattern hair loss in August 1991. However, it should not be used by pregnant or nursing women.

In his dermatological practice, Arthur P. Bertolino, M.D., Ph.D., director of the hair consultation unit at New York University, says that this lotion helps hair grow in 10 to 14 percent of the people who try it. He estimates that approximately 90 percent of the time, Rogaine at least slows down hair loss. (Minoxidil is also available in tablet form to treat severe high blood pressure. Oral minoxidil has a potential for serious side effects and is not approved to treat baldness.)

No one is certain yet just how topical minoxidil works to promote hair growth. "One theory is that it dilates the blood vessels, so it may stimulate nourishment of follicles," says Bihova. Alternatively, Rogaine may convert tiny hair follicles that produce peach fuzz into large hair follicles that produce normal-size hairs. Again, no one knows for sure.

What is certain is that, at least in men, Rogaine works better on patients who fit a certain profile: they've generally been bald for less than ten years, have bald spots on top of the head that are less than four inches in diameter, and they still have fine hairs in their balding areas. "The process begins very early," says Bihova. "I see 19-, 20-year-old males who have it."

The most common side effects with this medication are itching and skin irritation. Also, according to Bertolino, once you stop using it, any hair that grew as a result will fall out. Finally, the drug is expensive: in 1990, it cost about $600 a year to use it twice a day.

Transplants

Baldness can also be treated with hair transplants, in which plugs of "donor" follicles from the patient's scalp are used to fill the hairline. Although hair transplants work well in both men and women, the treatment tends to have a more dramatic effect on appearance in men with bald spots than it does on women with thinning hair.

"The less hair you have, the more drama in the change," says Robert Auerbach, M.D., associate professor of clinical dermatology at New York University School of Medicine. However, the American Hair Loss Council warns against attempting to replace lost hair with hair pieces sutured to the scalp. FDA has not approved any products specifically intended for this purpose; however, this does not preclude a physician from using sutures, which are approved devices, for this purpose. According to the council, although the procedure is legal, it can result in scars, infections, and even brain abscesses.

Another treatment for male-pattern baldness, hair implants made of high-density artificial fibers surgically implanted in the scalp, was banned by the FDA in 1984 because it causes infection. This is the only device FDA has ever banned.

Products That Don't Work

So-called "thinning hair supplements," "hair farming products," and "vasodilators" for the scalp will not promote hair growth, says Mike Mahoney, a spokesperson for the American Hair Loss Council.

Thinning hair supplements are nothing more than hair conditioners that temporarily make your hair feel or look a little thicker. The main ingredient in these products—polysorbate—is also found in many shampoos. Promotional materials for hair farming products claim that they will release hairs that are "trapped" in a bald scalp. Mahoney says these products, many of which are herbal preparations, can do no such thing. And so-called vasodilators do not increase the blood supply to the scalp and do not promote hair growth.

Everyday Hazards

While male- and female-pattern baldness results in permanent hair loss, other factors can cause temporary loss of hair. For instance, the drop in the level of estrogen at the end of pregnancy can cause a woman's hair to shed more readily. Two or three months after a woman stops taking birth control pills, she may experience the same effect, since birth control pills produce hormone changes that mimic pregnancy. A major physical stress, such as surgery, or a major emotional stress—positive or negative—can cause hair loss.

"I've seen women start losing their hair before getting married," says Bihova. Even jet lag can have a similar effect.

In most of these cases, the hormonal imbalance or stressful situation will correct itself, and the scalp will soon begin growing hair again. But, says Bihova, since most women are extremely upset by even a temporary hair loss, many dermatologists treat these conditions with either topical steroid preparations or localized injections of low doses of steroids. Bihova emphasizes that these are local, not systemic, injections of steroids; therefore, the shots do not have the same risk of dangerous side effects as systemic steroids. However, only a board-certified dermatologist should administer this treatment, she says.

The list of causes of temporary hair loss goes on: pressure on the scalp from wigs or hairdos that pull too tightly can cause it. A fever of 103 degrees Fahrenheit or more often causes hair loss six weeks to three months later. And some medications can cause a temporary loss. These include vitamin A derivatives such as Accutane, cough medicines with iodides, anti-ulcer drugs, some antibiotics, beta blockers, antidepressants and amphetamines, anti-arthritis drugs, blood thinners, some cholesterol-lowering agents, aspirin taken over long periods, some thyroid medications, and chemotherapy.

You Hair What You Eat?

Although nutrition does play a role in hair loss and in the overall health of your hair, only extreme nutritional deficiencies or excesses will cause hair loss. For instance, people with anorexia and bulimia may temporarily lose hair. So will others suffering from malnutrition.

"It's pretty rare in the United States," says Bertolino. "If someone was on a real strange, restrictive diet, it could happen to them."

Megadoses of some vitamins—particularly A and E—and an iron deficiency may lead to hair loss. People who claim they can determine which vitamins are lacking in your diet by analyzing your hair, however, are not speaking from a scientifically sound basis. The test used with this type of hair analysis—atomic absorption spectrophotometry—is a legitimate analytical chemistry method; however, used on hair, the results of this test do not correlate with nutritional status, says Shupack. "Because of the sociological importance of hair, a lot of people try to cash in on it," he says. "Hair analysis is all witchcraft as far as I'm concerned."

There are, however, a few legitimate hair tests for substances such as arsenic and lead.

For Beauty's Sake

Every time you shampoo, blow dry, perm, straighten, or dye your hair, you damage it slightly, says Bertolino. For the most part, hair can withstand this type of treatment. But overzealous beautifying can damage the hair fiber, resulting in many broken strands, and a frizzy, split-end look. For instance, if you bleach your hair and then have a bunch of perms done in a short time, you're heading for trouble.

Misuse of hair cosmetics can cause the hair to break as it comes out of the scalp, says Frances Storrs, M.D., professor of dermatology at the Oregon Health Sciences University. Permanent wave solutions break the bonds that hold hair together and then reform them. But with a perm that is not diluted right or not rinsed off properly, for instance, those bonds may not reform and the hair would soon fall out as a result. Fortunately, most professional hair dressers know how to use perms correctly, says Storrs.

Most hair dyes are not as irritating as permanent solutions, mostly because they do not break the bonds between hair fibers and are therefore not likely to cause a hair loss, she says. However, a severe allergic reaction to hair dye could cause hair loss.

"The allergy is pretty common, actually," says Storrs. Permanent solutions can also cause allergic reactions, though that's a rare side effect.

Other beauty-related manipulations of the hair can cause problems, too: hot irons, corn rows, and braids may bring on temporary or permanent hair loss. If the hair breaks often enough, the follicles may eventually not be able to produce normal hair, says Bihova. "If someone has a problem with thinning and excessive loss, we advise being gentle," she says. "Don't use rollers; don't use blow dryers on a hot setting; don't wear tight hair styles." Rough shampooing may accelerate any loss, though it's usually not a problem in people with healthy hair.

The Medical Side

Some hair loss is the result of a type of immune disorder known as alopecia areata—some 2.5 million people suffer from this condition in which antibodies attack the hair follicle, causing the hair to fall out. Alopecia areata often causes small, oval or circular areas of hair loss. However, in some forms of the condition, all the scalp hair falls out; in other forms, all body hair is lost. Although the loss is usually temporary, the condition can recur. Treatments include topical steroids or the use of chemicals to produce an allergic reaction to start the hair growing again.

Finally, chronic, systemic conditions—including one form of lupus, abnormal kidney and liver function, and hypothyroidism or hyperthyroidism—can affect the hair. If you're experiencing hair loss, see a doctor. He or she will want to order some basic blood tests to rule out any medical cause of the condition.

Sleepercize

If you're still reading (and starting to feel desperate) do what we did in school when we were totally bored. That's right: split ends. Do as many as you can. Count them as you do it—it's very soothing.

Your Boring Body

Golf Strategies

If golf is your game, you might want to turn to another selection lest this entry pique your interest and foil your plans for sleep. If you could care less about the links, read on, prospective sleeper! The combination of something that doesn't interest you and meticulous description is a guaranteed sedative. ●

ONE OF THE GREAT CHALLENGES of golf is that no two rounds will ever be the same, even if you play the same course over and over. Changing weather, seasons, and light are major factors that can affect your score and enjoyment of the game.

On the Range
If you are not familiar with the course, ask the pro what shots you are most likely to hit, based on your handicap. Ask if greens break a certain way, and if a course map is available, note these breaks with an arrow. Devote a majority of your practice time to these shots.

On the practice green, take three dimes and place one at ten, fifteen, and twenty yards away and hit five putts to each. This will visually concentrate your stroke and increase your confidence.

Clubs

There are a few adjustments to your club selection that can help you adapt to changing conditions.

Windy conditions: Add a 2-iron instead of a lob wedge or a seven wood.

Short, tight course: Consider leaving the driver out of the bag and add a third wedge.

Rain: Use a wedge with less bounce in the traps; also try hitting closer to the ball (2" versus 4-6").

Adapting to Rain

Rain will reduce distance or cause mis-shots. Rather than simply taking more club to counteract the rain, you should eliminate distractions.

- Keep the grips and hands dry using gloves on both hands.
- Plan a shot you can hit. Two hundred yards over water on a dry day may be okay, but in tough conditions two 100-yard shots will probably give you a better score.
- Take one more club than you normally would, and widen your stance.

Adapting to Wind

The most disruptive influence of wind is that it can cause doubt in the mind of golfers about their ability to hit the shot as planned. Most golfers should hit the shot they are used to, with one modification. Downwind, calculate the strength of wind adjustment (one club for each 10 mph). Reverse the process by adding clubs with a headwind.

- Play without a hat, to avoid distracting gusts.
- Play with eyeglasses, to prevent tearing and blowing dust or debris.
- Widen your stance on all shots (especially putts) for a firmer foundation.

Tedious Tips

Adapting to Temperature Shifts

Your head and your hands are most affected by temperature. With a round of golf lasting approximately 4 ½ hours, it is possible to experience dramatic temperature shifts.

Select a hat that provides sun protection but will not blow off in the wind. In extreme conditions, place a cotton washcloth inside for additional warmth, or to be soaked in water and applied to the back of your neck in hot weather.

Adapting to Changing Light

Depth perception, distance judgment, and breaks on greens are all greatly influenced by changing light. Photochromic eyeglasses give you the flexibility to play your best in any light. An additional option available on Transitions Lenses is anti-reflective coating. This feature reduces the glare from direct and indirect sunlight. Transitions Lenses also protect against harmful ultraviolet radiation (UV).

Using these tips and acquiring the proper tools to adapt your game to the challenges that nature presents will improve both your score and enjoyment on the course.

In Your Bag

In addition to the basics like a hat, rain suit, and towel, the following items can help with unanticipated problems on the course.

1. Transitions Lenses—Your eyes may be your best equipment. Photochromic plastic lenses that adjust their tint to light conditions will allow you to read greens and distances in bright sun or fading twilight. They also help protect your eyes from dust and pollen, and excessive tearing in windy or cold conditions.
2. Sunscreen—With a sun protection factor (SPF) of at least 15.
3. Insect spray.
4. Right- and left-hand golf gloves—Cold weather or rainy conditions make grips slippery.
5. Cloth Band Aids—Non-plastic type won't affect grip.

6. Ibuprofen—Inflammation reducer that is gentle on your stomach.
7. Small chamois—Absorbs large amounts of water to keep grips and gloves dry.

Tedious Tips

Exodus 22

Just in case you thought things were simpler in the old days, try on this venerable stack of proscriptions and directives straight from Jehovah Himself. More lulling passages from the Old Testament. Ⓨ

1: IF A MAN SHALL STEAL an ox, or a sheep, and kill it, or sell it; he shall restore five oxen for an ox, and four sheep for a sheep.

2: If a thief be found breaking up, and be smitten that he die, there shall no blood be shed for him.

3: If the sun be risen upon him, there shall be blood shed for him; for he should make full restitution; if he have nothing, then he shall be sold for his theft.

4: If the theft be certainly found in his hand alive, whether it be ox, or ass, or sheep; he shall restore double.

5: If a man shall cause a field or vineyard to be eaten, and shall put in his beast, and shall feed in another man's field; of the best of his own field, and of the best of his own vineyard, shall he make restitution.

6: If fire break out, and catch in thorns, so that the stacks of corn, or the standing corn, or the field, be consumed therewith; he that kindled the fire shall surely make restitution.

7: If a man shall deliver unto his neighbor money or stuff

to keep, and it be stolen out of the man's house; if the thief be found, let him pay double.

8: If the thief be not found, then the master of the house shall be brought unto the judges, to see whether he have put his hand unto his neighbor's goods.

9: For all manner of trespass, whether it be for ox, for ass, for sheep, for raiment, or for any manner of lost thing which another challengeth to be his, the cause of both parties shall come before the judges; and whom the judges shall condemn, he shall pay double unto his neighbor.

10: If a man deliver unto his neighbor an ass, or an ox, or a sheep, or any beast, to keep; and it die, or be hurt, or driven away, no man seeing it:

11: Then shall an oath of the LORD be between them both, that he hath not put his hand unto his neighbor's goods; and the owner of it shall accept thereof, and he shall not make it good.

12: And if it be stolen from him, he shall make restitution unto the owner thereof.

13: If it be torn in pieces, then let him bring it for witness, and he shall not make good that which was torn.

14: And if a man borrow ought of his neighbor, and it be hurt, or die, the owner thereof being not with it, he shall surely make it good.

15: But if the owner thereof be with it, he shall not make it good: if it be an hired thing, it came for his hire.

16: And if a man entice a maid that is not betrothed, and lie with her, he shall surely endow her to be his wife.

17: If her father utterly refuse to give her unto him, he shall pay money according to the dowry of virgins.

18: Thou shalt not suffer a witch to live.

19: Whosoever lieth with a beast shall surely be put to death.

20: He that sacrificeth unto any god, save unto the LORD only, he shall be utterly destroyed.

21: Thou shalt neither vex a stranger, nor oppress him: for ye were strangers in the land of Egypt.

22: Ye shall not afflict any widow, or fatherless child.

Soporific Classics

23: If thou afflict them in any wise, and they cry at all unto me, I will surely hear their cry;

24: And my wrath shall wax hot, and I will kill you with the sword; and your wives shall be widows, and your children fatherless.

25: If thou lend money to any of my people that is poor by thee, thou shalt not be to him as an usurer, neither shalt thou lay upon him usury.

26: If thou at all take thy neighbor's raiment to pledge, thou shalt deliver it unto him by that the sun goeth down:

27: For that is his covering only, it is his raiment for his skin: wherein shall he sleep? and it shall come to pass, when he crieth unto me, that I will hear; for I am gracious.

28: Thou shalt not revile the gods, nor curse the ruler of thy people.

29: Thou shalt not delay to offer the first of thy ripe fruits, and of thy liquors: the firstborn of thy sons shalt thou give unto me.

30: Likewise shalt thou do with thine oxen, and with thy sheep: seven days it shall be with his dam; on the eighth day thou shalt give it me.

31: And ye shall be holy men unto me: neither shall ye eat any flesh that is torn of beasts in the field; ye shall cast it to the dogs.

Sleepercize

Say you've made off with three oxen and five sheep from the house of your neighbor before sunrise, and you accidentally smite a widow and several orphans on your way out of the village on your way back to where you happen to be sleeping with someone who is not your spouse. What's the best you can hope for in these circumstances?

Can Insomnia Affect Your Quality of Life?

Hey, you're the one sitting there unable to sleep—what do you think? Is insomnia affecting the quality of your life? Damned right it is! And yet here is another well-funded study undertaken to prove the obvious. However, through a delightful coincidence this news report can improve your quality of life by putting you to sleep as you read it. Try it and see! Ⓨ

PEOPLE ROUTINELY LINK "quality of life" to satisfaction levels with their job, community, and family life, but a new study indicates that a person's quality of life can be significantly impacted by something even more basic—a good night's sleep.

The study reveals that people who suffer from insomnia—the inability to fall asleep or to stay asleep—experience a significant decline in their quality of life.

"This study highlights the importance of a good night's sleep upon almost every facet of our waking lives," said Dr. Gary Zammit of the Sleep Disorders Institute in New York, lead investigator of the study. "Patients and physicians alike should recognize that insomnia is more than a nuisance. It can be a serious condition that can significantly diminish a person's quality of life."

The study compared the completed questionnaires of 261

patients with insomnia to 101 persons without insomnia. Those with insomnia took longer to fall asleep, slept less during the night, and had less restful sleep than those patients without insomnia.

The study participants evaluated the following: body pain, general health, mental health, emotional and physical well-being, social and physical functioning, and vitality. In every category, participants with insomnia scored lower than those without insomnia.

People with insomnia also reported greater daytime sleepiness; higher levels of depression and anxiety; poor thinking ability, including concentration and problem-solving ability; poorer physical and mental well-being; and more disruptions in work and daily activities.

"Unfortunately, many of the side effects caused by insomnia that negatively impact a person's quality of life—such as grogginess, memory loss, and difficulty concentrating—are not always alleviated by sleep medications. In fact, some sleep medications cause these side effects," said Dr. Zammit. "This study underscores the need for better medications to help fight insomnia and improve the quality of life."

According to the National Sleep Foundation, insomnia affects nearly 84 million Americans each year. Insomnia may be caused by many things, such as a change in sleeping or daily environments; a new home or job; jet lag; a new work schedule; pain from arthritis, headache, menstrual cramps, or backache; stress or anxiety; or use of certain medications. If you suffer from insomnia, you may want to talk to your doctor about new treatments, exercises, and relaxation techniques.

Tedious Tips

Snow and Ice Control

Believe it or not, there is actually something more tedious than plowing through this collection of tips for keeping highways at their optimum condition during the winter. Just imagine having to write it! Ⓨ

More Efficient Winter Operations

Snow, sleet, and freezing rain can create treacherous driving conditions. To keep roads clear and safe for travel, highway agencies spend more than $2 billion every year on winter maintenance. Conventional winter maintenance operations involve deicing techniques—that is, sending plows and trucks loaded with salt and other materials to clear the roadways after a storm has begun. Although effective, this strategy is costly and labor intensive, and can cause unnecessary harm to the environment.

Now there is a better way. The Strategic Highway Research Program (SHRP) found that by switching from traditional deicing techniques to an anti-icing strategy coupled with a road weather information system (RWIS), highway agencies can

- Slash their winter maintenance costs.
- Improve travel conditions.
- Help protect the environment.

SHRP also evaluated the snow fence, a simple technique more than 100 years old, and found it effective at preventing blowing and drifting snow from closing roads and reducing visibility.

Timing Is Everything

An anti-icing strategy involves applying salt or other chemicals that lower the freezing point of water to the pavement before a storm hits. When sleet, freezing rain, or snow begins to fall, the freezing-point depressant will prevent ice from forming on the pavement. Instead of freezing over, the pavement stays wet or slushy—which means travel is safer and clean-up is easier.

Anti-icing technologies have been around for a while, but they have not been extensively used because highway agencies lacked the means to collect and analyze information telling them precisely when and where chemicals should be applied. That's where the RWIS comes in.

An RWIS consists of a network of monitoring stations located along primary roads and at potential trouble spots, such as bridges. At each RWIS station, sensors collect data on

- pavement and atmospheric conditions, including temperature;
- the rate of falling snow, rain, or sleet; and
- the amount of chemicals remaining on the pavement from previous applications.

These measurements are transmitted to a central computer, where they are combined with meteorological information from the National Weather Service and with other, more localized forecasts. The information is then used to predict when and where precipitation is likely to freeze to the pavement and when and where crews should be sent.

An RWIS allows highway agencies to make more informed decisions about where and when to deploy materials, crews, and equipment. Not only does this help the highway agency stay ahead of the storm, but it also means less unnecessary crew standby time, which cuts overtime costs. Salt and other chemicals are more judiciously applied, which means less chemical runoff into streams and wetlands and onto farmland.

Many states are already using anti-icing strategies. Nevada, for example, has found that maintenance efforts are more effective and staff and equipment requirements are reduced with RWIS and anti-icing strategies. Nevada expects its expanding RWIS system to

- Provide motorists and shippers with safer, more reliable travel conditions.
- Save $7 million in labor, materials, and other costs over the next 25 years.
- Protect the environment by reducing the amount of chemicals and abrasives used.

In Colorado, an anti-icing/RWIS strategy is helping to improve air quality. Sand and other abrasives applied to pavements are responsible for about 20 percent of Denver's persistent winter air quality problems. Anti-icing strategies are reducing sand use without sacrificing safe travel conditions.

Keeping the Snow at Bay

Snow fences work by trapping blowing snow, keeping it from piling up or drifting across roadways. In southeastern Idaho, for example, snow fences strategically placed along Highway 37 keep the road open even in severe winds. "Highway 37 is the only route between American Falls and Rockland, so a road closure is serious business, since this is a school bus, mail, and commercial route," says Brian Mansfield of the Idaho Transportation Department. Before the highway agency placed snow fences along the roadway, blowing snow forced the road to be closed several times every winter, and each closure required 8 to 10 hours of labor and equipment time to clear.

Saving Money, Time, and Materials

A recent economic study by the Texas Transportation Institute (TTI) found that the SHRP winter maintenance technologies

Tedious Tips

could save millions of dollars. According to TTI, if highway agencies adopt anti-icing strategies and RWIS, they could cut winter maintenance costs by $55 million to $108 million annually, depending on how quickly they implement the technologies. Because travel conditions would be safer, motorists could save $229 million to $447 million annually in user costs.

Nutrition Guidelines

No doubt about it, eating is much more enjoyable to do than to read about. For the die-hard insomniacs among us, we offer this gem from the FDA to plunge you into deep slumber. That is, if you aren't lured into the kitchen for a late-night snack instead.

THESE GUIDELINES PROVIDE ADVICE for healthy Americans age 2 years and over about food choices that promote health and prevent disease. To meet the Dietary Guidelines for Americans, choose a diet with most of the calories from grain products, vegetables, fruits, lowfat milk products, lean meats, fish, poultry, and dry beans. Choose fewer calories from fats and sweets.

Eating is one of life's greatest pleasures

Food choices depend on history, culture, and environment, as well as on energy and nutrient needs. People also eat foods for enjoyment. Family, friends, and beliefs play a major role in the ways people select foods and plan meals. This booklet describes some of the many different and pleasurable ways to combine foods to make healthful diets.

Diet is important to health at all stages of life

Many genetic, environmental, behavioral, and cultural factors can affect health. Understanding family history of disease or risk factors—body weight and fat distribution, blood pressure, and blood cholesterol, for example—can help people make more informed decisions about actions that can improve health prospects. Food choices are among the most pleasurable and effective of these actions.

Healthful diets help children grow, develop, and do well in school. They enable people of all ages to work productively and feel their best. Food choices also can help to reduce the risk for chronic diseases, such as heart disease, certain cancers, diabetes, stroke, and osteoporosis, that are leading causes of death and disability among Americans. Good diets can reduce major risk factors for chronic diseases—factors such as obesity, high blood pressure, and high blood cholesterol.

Foods contain energy, nutrients, and other components that affect health

People require energy and certain other essential nutrients. These nutrients are essential because the body cannot make them and must obtain them from food. Essential nutrients include vitamins, minerals, certain amino acids, and certain fatty acids. Foods also contain other components such as fiber that are important for health. Although each of these food components has a specific function in the body, all of them together are required for overall health. People need calcium to build and maintain strong bones, for example, but many other nutrients also are involved.

The carbohydrates, fats, and proteins in food supply energy, which is measured in calories. Carbohydrates and proteins provide about 4 calories per gram. Fat contributes more than twice as much—about 9 calories per gram. Alcohol, although not a nutrient, also supplies energy —about 7 calories per gram. Foods that are high in fat are also high in calories. However, many lowfat or nonfat foods can also be high in calories.

Physical activity fosters a healthful diet

Calorie needs vary by age and level of activity. Many older adults need less food, in part due to decreased activity, relative to younger, more active individuals. People who are trying to lose weight and eating little food may need to select more nutrient-dense foods in order to meet their nutrient needs in a satisfying diet. Nearly all Americans need to be more active, because a sedentary lifestyle is unhealthful. Increasing the calories spent in daily activities helps to maintain health and allows people to eat a nutritious and enjoyable diet.

What is a healthful diet?

Healthful diets contain the amounts of essential nutrients and calories needed to prevent nutritional deficiencies and excesses. Healthful diets also provide the right balance of carbohydrate, fat, and protein to reduce risks for chronic diseases, and are a part of a full and productive lifestyle. Such diets are obtained from a variety of foods that are available, affordable, and enjoyable.

The Recommended Dietary Allowances refer to nutrients

Recommended Dietary Allowances (RDAs) represent the amounts of nutrients that are adequate to meet the needs of most healthy people. Although people with average nutrient requirements likely eat adequately at levels below the RDAs, diets that meet RDAs are almost certain to ensure intake of enough essential nutrients by most healthy people.

The Dietary Guidelines describe food choices that will help you meet these recommendations. Like the RDAs, the Dietary Guidelines apply to diets consumed over several days and not to single meals or foods.

The Dietary Guidelines describe food choices that promote good health

The Dietary Guidelines are designed to help Americans choose diets that will meet nutrient requirements, promote health, support active lives, and reduce chronic disease risks. Research has shown that certain diets raise risks for chronic diseases. Such diets are high in fat, saturated fat, cholesterol, and salt and they contain more calories than the body uses. They are also low in grain products, vegetables, fruit, and fiber. This bulletin helps

Your Boring Body

you choose foods, meals, and diets that can reduce chronic disease risks.

Food labels and the Food Guide Pyramid are tools to help you make food choices
The Food Guide Pyramid and the Nutrition Facts Label serve as educational tools to put the Dietary Guidelines into practice. The Pyramid translates the RDAs and the Dietary Guidelines into the kinds and amounts of food to eat each day. The Nutrition Facts Label is designed to help you select foods for a diet that will meet the Dietary Guidelines. Most processed foods now include nutrition information. However, nutrition labels are not required for foods like coffee and tea (which contain no significant amounts of nutrients), certain ready-to-eat foods like unpackaged deli and bakery items, and restaurant food. Labels are also voluntary for many raw foods—your grocer may supply this information for the fish, meat, poultry, and raw fruits and vegetables that are consumed most frequently. Use the Nutrition Facts Label to choose a healthful diet.

Eat a variety of foods
To obtain the nutrients and other substances needed for good health, vary the foods you eat.

Foods contain combinations of nutrients and other healthful substances. No single food can supply all nutrients in the amounts you need. For example, oranges provide vitamin C but no vitamin B12; cheese provides vitamin B12 but no vitamin C. To make sure you get all of the nutrients and other substances needed for health, choose the recommended number of daily servings from each of the five major food groups displayed in the Food Guide Pyramid.

Use foods from the base of the Food Guide Pyramid as the foundation of your meals
Americans do choose a wide variety of foods. However, people often choose higher or lower amounts from some food groups than suggested in the Food Guide Pyramid. The Pyramid shows

that foods from the grain products group, along with vegetables and fruits, are the basis of healthful diets. Enjoy meals that have rice, pasta, potatoes, or bread at the center of the plate, accompanied by other vegetables and fruit, and lean and low-fat foods from the other groups. Limit fats and sugars added in food preparation and at the table.

Choose foods from each of five food groups

The Food Guide Pyramid illustrates the importance of balance among food groups in a daily eating pattern. Most of the daily servings of food should be selected from the largest food groups that are closest to the base of the Pyramid.

- Choose most of your foods from the grain products group (6-11 servings), the vegetable group (3-5 servings), and the fruit group (2-4 servings).
- Eat moderate amounts of foods from the milk group (2-3 servings) and the meat and beans group (2-3 servings).
- Choose sparingly foods that provide few nutrients and are high in fat and sugars.

NOTE: A range of servings is given for each food group. The smaller number is for people who consume about 1,600 calories a day, such as many sedentary women. The larger number is for those who consume about 2,800 calories a day, such as active men.

What counts as a "serving"?

Some of the serving sizes are smaller than what you might usually eat. For example, many people eat a cup or more of pasta in a meal, which equals two or more servings. So, it is easy to eat the number of servings recommended.

GRAIN PRODUCTS GROUP (BREAD, CEREAL, RICE, AND PASTA)
- 1 slice of bread
- 1 ounce of ready-to-eat cereal
- ½ cup of cooked cereal, rice, or pasta

Your Boring Body

VEGETABLE GROUP
- 1 cup of raw leafy vegetables
- ½ cup of other vegetables—cooked or chopped raw
- ¾ cup of vegetable juice

FRUIT GROUP
- 1 medium apple, banana, orange
- ½ cup of chopped, cooked, or canned fruit
- ¾ cup of fruit juice

MILK GROUP (MILK, YOGURT, AND CHEESE)
- 1 cup of milk or yogurt
- 1 ½ ounces of natural cheese
- 2 ounces of processed cheese

MEAT AND BEANS GROUP (MEAT, POULTRY, FISH, DRY BEANS, EGGS, AND NUTS)
- 2-3 ounces of cooked lean meat, poultry, or fish
- ½ cup of cooked dry beans or 1 egg counts as 1 ounce of lean meat.
- Two tablespoons of peanut butter or ⅓ cup of nuts counts as 1 ounce of meat.

Some foods fit into more than one group. Dry beans, peas, and lentils can be counted as servings in either the meat and beans group or vegetable group. These "cross over" foods can be counted as servings from either one or the other group, but not both. Serving sizes indicated here are those used in the Food Guide Pyramid and based on both suggested and usually consumed portions necessary to achieve adequate nutrient intake. They differ from serving sizes on the Nutrition Facts label, which reflect portions usually consumed.

Choose different foods within each food group
You can achieve a healthful, nutritious eating pattern with many combinations of foods from the five major food groups. Choosing a variety of foods within and across food groups improves

dietary patterns because foods within the same group have different combinations of nutrients and other beneficial substances. For example, some vegetables and fruits are good sources of vitamin C or vitamin A, while others are high in folate; still others are good sources of calcium or iron. Choosing a variety of foods within each group also helps to make your meals more interesting from day to day.

Some good sources of calcium:*
- Most foods in the milk group**
- Milk and dishes made with milk, such as puddings and soups made with milk
- Cheeses such as Mozzarella, Cheddar, Swiss, and Parmesan
- Yogurt
- Canned fish with soft bones such as sardines, anchovies, and salmon**
- Dark-green leafy vegetables, such as kale, mustard greens, turnip greens, and pak-choi
- Tofu, if processed with calcium sulfate. Read the labels.
- Tortillas made from lime-processed corn. Read the labels.
  Read food labels for brand-specific information.
  **Some foods in this group are high in fat, cholesterol, or both. Choose lower fat, lower cholesterol foods most often. Read the labels.*

Some good sources of iron:*
- Meats—beef, pork, lamb, and liver and other organ meats**
- Poultry—chicken, duck, and turkey, especially dark meat; liver**
- Fish—shellfish, like clams, mussels, and oysters; sardines; anchovies; and other fish**
- Leafy greens of the cabbage family, such as broccoli, kale, turnip greens, collards
- Legumes, such as lima beans and green peas; dry beans and peas, such as pinto beans, black-eyed peas, and canned baked beans
- Yeast-leavened whole-wheat bread and rolls

Your Boring Body

- Iron-enriched white bread, pasta, rice, and cereals. Read the labels.

Does not include complete list of examples. You can obtain additional information from "Good Sources of Nutrients," USDA, January 1990. Also read food labels for brand-specific information.

**Some foods in this group are high in fat, cholesterol, or both. Choose lower fat, lower cholesterol foods most often. Read the labels.*

Enriched and fortified foods have essential nutrients added to them

National policy requires that specified amounts of nutrients be added to enrich some foods. For example, enriched flour and bread contain added thiamin, riboflavin, niacin, and iron; skim milk, lowfat milk, and margarine are usually enriched with vitamin A; and milk is usually enriched with vitamin D. Fortified foods may have one or several nutrients added in extra amounts. The number and quantity of nutrients added vary among products. Fortified foods may be useful for meeting special dietary needs. Read the ingredient list to know which nutrients are added to foods. How these foods fit into your total diet will depend on the amounts you eat and the other foods you consume.

Where do vitamin, mineral, and fiber supplements fit in?

Supplements of vitamins, minerals, or fiber also may help to meet special nutritional needs. However, supplements do not supply all of the nutrients and other substances present in foods that are important to health. Supplements of some nutrients taken regularly in large amounts are harmful. Daily vitamin and mineral supplements at or below the Recommended Dietary Allowances are considered safe, but are usually not needed by people who eat the variety of foods depicted in the Food Guide Pyramid.

Sometimes supplements are needed to meet specific nutrient requirements. For example, older people and others with little exposure to sunlight may need a vitamin D supplement. Women of childbearing age may reduce the risk of certain birth defects by consuming folate-rich foods or folic acid supplements. Iron supplements are recommended for pregnant women. However, because foods contain many nutrients and other substances that promote health, the use of supplements cannot substitute for proper food choices.

Advice for today
Enjoy eating a variety of foods. Get the many nutrients your body needs by choosing among the varied foods you enjoy from these groups: grain products, vegetables, fruits, milk and milk products, protein-rich plant foods (beans, nuts), and protein-rich animal foods (lean meat, poultry, fish, and eggs). Remember to choose lean and lowfat foods and beverages most often. Many foods you eat contain servings from more than one food group. For example, soups and stews may contain meat, beans, noodles, and vegetables.

Balance the food you eat with physical activity—maintain or improve your weight
Many Americans gain weight in adulthood, increasing their risk for high blood pressure, heart disease, stroke, diabetes, certain types of cancer, arthritis, breathing problems, and other illness. Therefore, most adults should not gain weight. If you are overweight and have one of these problems, you should try to lose weight, or at the very least, not gain weight. If you are uncertain about your risk of developing a problem associated with overweight, you should consult a health professional.

How to maintain your weight
In order to stay at the same body weight, people must balance the amount of calories in the foods and drinks they consume with the amount of calories the body uses. Physical activity is an important way to use food energy. Most Americans spend much of their working day in activities that require little energy. In addition, many Americans of all ages now spend a lot of leisure time each day being inactive, for example, watching television or working at a computer. To burn calories, devote less time to sedentary activities like sitting. Spend more time in activities like

Your Boring Body

walking to the store or around the block. Use stairs rather than elevators. Less sedentary activity and more vigorous activity may help you reduce body fat and disease risk.

To increase calorie expenditure by physical activity
Remember to accumulate 30 minutes or more of moderate physical activity on most—preferably all—days of the week.

Examples of moderate physical activities for healthy U.S. adults:

- walking briskly (3–4 miles per hour)
- conditioning or general calisthenics
- home care, general cleaning
- racket sports such as table tennis
- mowing lawn, power mower
- golf—pulling cart or carrying clubs
- home repair, painting
- fishing, standing/casting
- jogging
- swimming (moderate effort)
- cycling, moderate speed (10 miles per hour or less)
- gardening
- canoeing leisurely (2.0–3.9 miles per hour)
- dancing

NASA Fatigue
Countermeasures

Perhaps as a result of reading space launch transcripts (see page 90), NASA determined that falling asleep at the controls of an enormous, million-dollar aircraft was probably not a good thing. As a result, they produced an anti-fatigue document that may inadvertently produce the opposite effect. Ⓨ

IN 1980, RESPONDING to a Congressional request, NASA Ames Research Center created a program to examine whether "there is a safety problem of uncertain magnitude, due to transmeridian flying and a potential problem due to fatigue in association with various factors found in air transport operations." The NASA Ames Fatigue/Jet Lag Program was created to collect systematic, scientific information on fatigue, sleep, circadian rhythms, and performance in flight operations. Three program goals were established and continue to guide research efforts:

- to determine the extent of fatigue, sleep loss, and circadian disruption in flight operations
- to determine the impact of these factors on flight crew performance
- to develop and evaluate countermeasures to mitigate the

adverse effects of these factors and maximize flight crew performance and alertness

Since 1980, studies have been conducted in a variety of aviation environments, controlled laboratory environments, as well as a full-mission flight simulation study. In 1991, the name of the program was changed to the Fatigue Countermeasures Program to provide a greater emphasis on the development and evaluation of countermeasures.

Information on the following highlights some of the Program's previous research findings, current activities, publications, and point of contact information.

Planned Cockpit Rest

Anecdotal, observational, and self-report sources have indicated that to compensate physiologically for sleep loss and circadian disruption sleep can occur on the flight deck. It is unclear from available data how often these are planned naps or occur spontaneously in response to the sleep loss and circadian disruption. Inflight rest on the flight deck is not sanctioned under current federal regulations. In consideration of the available information regarding rest on the flight deck, the first test of an operational fatigue countermeasure was conducted. A NASA/FAA study examined the effectiveness of a planned cockpit rest period to maintain and/or improve subsequent performance and alertness in long-haul nonaugmented international flights (nonaugmented = only primary crew required; augmented = extra crew needed when over certain flying times).

A regularly scheduled 12 day, 8 leg trip schedule that involved multiple transpacific crossings was chosen. The flight lengths averaged just over 9 hours followed by about 25 hours of layover. Prior to, during, and after the 12 day trip schedule, crew members completed Pilot Daily Logbooks documenting sleep and duty times and other activities and wore actigraphs on their nondominant wrist. The middle 4 legs of the trip schedule were studied intensively. Measures during the study flight legs included continuous physiological monitoring of EEG (brain) and EOG (eye movement) activity using a Medilog recorder. An extensive scientific literature demonstrates that self-reports of sleep (e.g., time to fall asleep, total sleep time) do not accurately reflect physiological activity. Therefore, it was critical to document the amount of physiological sleep obtained. The continuous EEG and EOG recordings during the wakefulness period were also used to assess physiological sleepiness. The Psychomotor Vigilance Task (PVT) was used as a measure of vigilance performance/sustained attention. Pilots also gave self-report ratings of alertness and mood at predetermined times throughout the flight. Two NASA researchers traveled with the crews to implement the procedures and collect data. The 3-person B747 volunteer crew members were randomly assigned to either a Rest Group or No-Rest Group. Each Rest Group crew member (12 Subjects) had a 40 minute rest opportunity during the cruise, low workload portion of flights over water. Crew members rested one at a time on a prearranged rotation while the other two crew members maintained the flight. The No-Rest Group crew members (9 Subjects) had a 40 minute control period identified when they were instructed to continue their regular flight activities. Specific safety and procedural guidelines were used during the study.

The first question was whether pilots would be able to sleep given a planned rest opportunity in their cockpit seat. The Rest Group crew members slept on 93% of the rest opportunities. On average, they fell asleep in 5.6 minutes and slept for about 26 minutes. If pilots were able to nap, it was also critical to determine whether there was a benefit associated with this sleep. This was determined by examining the vigilance performance measure and indicators of physiological sleepiness. As expected, the No-Rest Control Group showed performance decrements at the end of flights compared to the beginning of flights, on night flights versus day flights, and on the fourth study leg compared to the first study leg. However, the positive effects of the brief nap were demonstrated in the Rest Group as they maintained consistently good performance at the end of flights, on night flights, and on the fourth study leg. The naps were associated with the subsequent maintenance of initial performance levels compared to the decrements observed in the No-Rest Group. Physiological sleepiness was examined by evaluating the subtle EEG and EOG changes that occur indicating state liability. Previous research has demonstrated that physiological sleepiness is associated with the occurrence of EEG alpha or theta and/or EOG slow eye movements. These physiological events are associated with decreased performance. Microevents indicative of physiological sleepiness (the occurrence of EEG alpha or theta and/or EOG slow eye movements), lasting 5 seconds or longer, were identified during the last 90 minutes of flight, including descent and landing, for both study groups. Overall, the No-Rest Group had microevents (average of 6.37) indicative of physiological sleepiness at a rate twice that of the Rest Group (average of 2.90 microevents).

This brief "NASA nap" appeared to act as an acute inflight operational safety valve and did not affect the cumulative sleep debt observed in 85% of the crew members. The Rest Group crew members were able to obtain sleep during the rest opportunity and this nap was associated with improved performance and alertness compared to the No-Rest Control Group. This was the first empirical test of a fatigue countermeasure conducted in an operational aviation setting that combined physiological, performance, and subjective measures.

Again, not only are the results scientifically interesting but they can be transferred directly into operational considerations regarding planned rest. Based partly on the results of this NASA/FAA study, an industry/government working group has drafted an Advisory Circular (AC) for Controlled Rest on the Flight Deck. The AC outlines specific guidelines for the development and implementation of a program for controlled rest on the flight deck. It should be noted that controlled rest is only one acute inflight countermeasure and is not the panacea for all of the sleep loss and circadian disruption engendered by long-haul flight operations.

Practical Palmistry

You may have thought pursuing a career as a palm reader required only a shabby storefront, a neon sign reading "PSYCHIC," and a colorful assortment of headscarves. But you'd be so very wrong. There is a great, numbingly long body of knowledge to be absorbed before you glimpse the future in someone's mitt. Here's one sure prediction: read this and you will become verrry sleepy. ⓨ

Fingers

The term Palmistry is familiar to everyone, and its significance is well understood; but the exact meanings of its constituent parts, Chirognomony and Chiromancy, and their relative value, are known only to Palmistry's most zealous devotees. Chirognomony is the study of the form of the hand, while Chiromancy is the study of the lines of the palm.

For correct judgment these must be considered together, but their spheres are rather different.

Chirognomony deals almost entirely with character, and contains seven points of study:

1. The length of the finger
2. The knots on the fingers
3. Shape of the finger tips

4. Length of the phalanges
5. Shape of the nails
6. The thumb, which holds so important a place in palmistry as to make it a study by itself
7. Mounts at the root of the fingers, or on the side of the hand

Speaking generally, long fingers, by which I mean fingers long in proportion to the palm, show a love of detail, apparent in everything, from the painting of a picture to the adornment of a dinner-table; in some cases it becomes a ruling passion, and I have known people in whom this love of detail is highly developed, whose feelings towards their friends were completely changed by the sloppiness of a pair of shoes, or an untoward putting of hands in pockets. It should always be remembered that the granting of a favor by a long-fingered man will be dependent on the impression made by look, manner, and dress.

Excessively long fingers often show a love of gambling, especially when the second and third are of equal length; but to determine this, one should consult the line of head. In some badly-endowed hands these fingers show a grasping disposition, restrained by no over-particularity.

Short fingers show a person who takes things en masse, who simply cannot be bothered with the details and small events of life; short-fingered people are generally less impulsive than their longer-fingered brethren and less able to abstract themselves from their material surroundings, on which they are often very dependent. Mental anxiety, however, rarely troubles them, and they will patiently wait long-delayed news of absent friends, though driven frantic if a luncheon is late or tea cold.

Mr. A. R. Craig, in his *Book on the Hand*, gives, among other quotations from the *Old Fathers of Palmistry*, an excellent danger-signal to husbands. He says, "Observe the finger of Mercury—that is, the little finger—if the end exceed the joint of the third finger, such a man will rule his house, and his wife will be pleasing and obedient to him; but if it be short, and reach not the joint, he will have a shrew, and she will wear the breeches." The joint referred to is, of course, the one nearest the nail.

Knots and Fingertips

In connection with knots, Desbarrolles talks much about "Astral Fluid," any reference to which would be sheer waste of time, so I will merely state that, as natural indications of character, they demand most careful consideration.

A knot on the first joint, nearest the nail, shows love of philosophy; a knot on the second joint, love of order, which may be shown by bringing into shape involved writings or companies, or merely by exactness in everyday things. Where both knots are found, orderly reasonableness reduces all philosophical speculation to calm consideration of known facts, the positive and useful conquering of the imaginative and beautiful. If an artist has these two knots, he will be realistic in the extreme, and will employ his talent in depicting domestic details, only fit for Aunt Louisa's storybooks. A man with both knots and square fingers will probably be a mathematician, and become a slave to rule and symmetry. Fingers utterly devoid of knots have no order, although with square tips, there is love of its results. Such people like their rooms to be models of neatness, and expect to have all their properties within reach, but they make hay in their wardrobes, and havoc in their domestics' hearts.

The study of fingertips is so closely connected with that of knots, that I find I must combine the two and at once mention the indications given by the ends of the fingers. Observe, however, that these indications vary according to the finger, pointed tips of the first and the little meaning totally different things, but into these infinite variations it is impossible to enter here.

Sleepercize

Stare at your right hand. Slowly trace the lines on it. Get in touch with your psychic abilities. What are your lines telling you about your life? (Go ahead and fantasize) . . . fame and fortune, immortality, the love affair of the century.

Title

Preventing Foot Trouble

Your humble feet. They put up with a lot, don't they, carrying you around on their soles all day long. Still, you can't deny it: feet are not a riveting subject. Take a load off those poor dogs and read this piece about the common ailments of your pedal extremities. Ⓨ

IMPROVING THE CIRCULATION of blood to the feet can help prevent problems. Exposure to cold temperatures or water, pressure from shoes, long periods of sitting, or smoking can reduce flood flow to the feet. Even sitting with your legs crossed or wearing tight, elastic garters or socks can affect circulation. On the other hand, raising the feet, standing up and stretching, walking, and other forms of exercise promote good circulation. Gentle massage and warm foot baths can also help increase circulation to the feet.

Wearing comfortable shoes that fit well can prevent many foot ailments. Foot width may increase with age. Always have your feet measured when buying shoes. The upper part of the shoes should be made of a soft, flexible material to match the shape of your foot. Shoes made of leather can reduce the possibility of skin irritations. Soles should provide solid footing and not be slippery. Thick soles lessen pressure when walking on hard surfaces. Low-heeled shoes are more comfortable, safer, and less damaging than high-heeled shoes.

Common Foot Problems

Fungal and bacterial conditions—including athlete's foot—occur because the feet are usually enclosed in a dark, damp, warm environment. These infections cause redness, blisters, peeling, and itching. If not treated promptly, an infection may become chronic and difficult to cure. To prevent these conditions, keep the feet—especially the area between the toes—clean and dry and expose the feet to air whenever possible. If you are prone to fungal infections, you may want to dust your feet daily with a fungicidal powder.

Dry skin can cause itching and burning feet. Use mild soap sparingly and a body lotion on your legs and feet every day. The best moisturizers contain petroleum jelly or lanolin. Be cautious about adding oils to bath water since they can make the feet and bathtub very slippery.

Corns and calluses are caused by the friction and pressure of bony areas rubbing against shoes. A podiatrist or a physician can determine the cause of this condition and can suggest treatment, which may include getting better-fitting shoes or special pads. Over-the-counter medicines contain acids that destroy the tissue but do not treat the cause. These medicines can sometimes reduce the need for surgery. Treating corns or calluses yourself may be harmful, especially if you have diabetes or poor circulation.

Warts are skin growths caused by viruses. They are sometimes painful and, if untreated, may spread. Since over-the-counter preparations rarely cure warts, get professional care. A doctor can apply medicines, burn or freeze the wart off, or remove the wart surgically.

Bunions develop when big toe joints are out of line and become swollen and tender. Bunions may be caused by poor-fitting shoes that press on a deformity or an inherited weakness in the foot. If a bunion is not severe, wearing shoes cut wide at the instep and toes may provide relief. Protective pads can also cushion the painful area. Bunions can be treated by applying or injecting certain drugs, using whirlpool baths, or sometimes having surgery.

Ingrown toenails occur when a piece of the nail breaks the skin. This is usually caused by improperly trimmed nails. Ingrown toenails are especially common in the large toes. A podiatrist or doctor can remove the part of the nail that is cutting into the skin. This will allow the area to heal. Ingrown toenails can usually be avoided by cutting the toenail straight across and level with the top of the toe.

Hammertoe is caused by shortening the tendons that control toe movements. The toe knuckle is usually enlarged, drawing the toe back. Over time, the joint enlarges and stiffens as it rubs against shoes. Your balance may be affected. Hammertoe is treated by wearing shoes and stockings with plenty of toe room. In advanced cases, surgery may be recommended.

Spurs are calcium growths that develop on bones of the feet. They are caused by muscle strain in the feet and are irritated by standing for long periods of time, wearing badly fitting shoes, or being overweight. Sometimes they are completely painless, but at other times the pain can be severe. Treatments for spurs include using proper foot support, heel pads, heel cups, or other recommendations by a podiatrist or surgeon.

John Glenn's
"Friendship 7" Transcript

In 1962 NASA put the first American in space, and produced careful transcripts of the radio transmission between astronaut John Glenn in the capsule and mission control back on earth. It's your good fortune that the results are as enervating as a visit to the DMV. ⓨ

FEBRUARY 20, 1962, selected pages

04 37 18   This is Friendship 7, going to manual control.

04 37 21   Ah, Roger, Friendship 7.

04 37 23   This is banging in and out here; I'll just control it manually.

04 37 25   Roger.

04 37 48   Friendship 7, Guaymas Cap Com reading you loud and clear.

04 37 51   Roger, Guaymas, read out loud and clear also.

04 38 06   *(Texas)* Friendship 7, Friendship 7, this is Texas Com Tech. Do you read? Over.

04 38 10   Roger, Texas, go ahead.

04 38 13   Ah, Roger. Reading you 5 square. Stand by for Texas Cap Com.

04 38 16   Roger.

04 38 25   This is Texas Cap Com, Friendship 7. We are rec-

ommending that you leave the retropackage on through the entire reentry. This means that you will have to override the 05g switch which is expected to occur at 04 43 _ 3. This also means that you will have to manually retract the scope. Do you read?

04 38 49   This is Friendship 7. What is the reason for this? Do you have any reason? Over.

04 38 58   Not at this time; this is the judgment of Cape Flight.

04 38 58   Ah, Roger. Say again your instructions please. Over.

04 39 01   We are recommending that the retropackage not, I say again, not be jettisoned. This means that you will have to override the 05g switch which is expected to occur at 04 43 53. This is approximately four-and-a-half minutes from now. This also means that you will have to retract the scope manually. Do you understand?

04 39 25   Ah, Roger, understand. I will have to make a manual 05g entry when it occurs, and bring the scope in, ah, manually. Is that affirm?

04 39 35   That is affirmative, Friendship 7.

04 39 39   Ah, Roger.

04 39 42   This is Friendship 7, going to reentry attitude, then, in that case.

04 40 00   Friendship 7, Cape flight will give you the reasons for this action when you are in view.

04 40 06   Ah, Roger. Ah, Roger. Friendship 7.

04 40 09   Everything down here on the ground looks okay.

04 40 12   Ah, Roger. This is Friendship 7.

04 40 14   Confirm your attitudes.

04 40 16   Roger.

04 40 23   *(Canaveral)* Ah, Friendship 7, this is Cape. Over.

04 40 25   Go ahead, Cape. Friend 7.

04 40 27   Ah, recommend you go to reentry attitude and retract the scope manually at this time.

04 40 32   Ah, Roger, retracting scope manually.

04 40 36   While you're doing that, we are not sure whether or not your landing bag has deployed. We feel it is possible to reenter with the retropackage on. Ah, we see no difficulty at this time in that type of reentry. Over.

04 40 51   Ah, Roger, understand.

04 41 10   Seven, this is Cape. Over.

04 41 12   Go ahead, Cape. Friendship 7.

04 41 15   Estimating 05g at 04 44.

04 41 21   Ah, Roger.

04 41 23   You override 05g at that time.

04 41 31   Ah, Roger. Friendship 7.

04 41 33   This is Friendship 7. I'm on straight manual control at present time. This was, ah, still kicking in and out of orientation mode, mainly in yaw, ah, following retrofire, so I am on straight manual now. I'll back it up—on reentry.

04 41 45   —on reentry.

04 41 47   Say again.

04 41 50   Standby.

04 41 53   This is Friendship 7. Ah, going to fly-by-wire. I'm down to about 15 percent on manual.

04 42 00   Ah, Roger. You're going to use fly-by-wire for reentry and we recommend that you do the best you can to keep a zero angle during reentry. Over.

04 42 09   Ah, Roger. Friendship 7.

04 42 13   This is Friendship 7. I'm on fly-by-wire, back it up with manual. Over.

04 42 18   Roger, understand.

04 42 29   Ah, Seven, this is Cape. The weather in the recovery area is excellent, 3-foot waves, only one-tenth cloud coverage, 10 miles visibility.

04 42 39   Ah, Roger. Friendship 7.

04 42 47   Ah, Seven, this is Cape. Over.

04 42 49   Go ahead, Cape, you're ground, you are going out.

04 42 52   We recommend that you —

04 43 16   This is Friendship 7. I think the pack just let go.

Great (Dull) Moments in History

04 43 39   This is Friendship 7. A real fireball outside.

04 44 20   Hello, Cape. Friendship 7. Over.

04 45 18   Hello, Cape. Friendship 7. Over.

04 45 43   Hello, Cape. Friendship 7. Do you receive? Over.

04 46 20   Hello, Cape. Friendship 7. Do you receive? Over.

04 47 18   —How do you read? Over.

04 47 20   Loud and clear; how me?

04 47 22   Roger, reading you loud and clear. How are you doing?

04 47 25   Oh, pretty good.

04 47 30   Roger. Your impact point is within one mile of the up-range destroyer.

04 47 34   Ah, Roger.

04 47 35   —Over

04 47 36   Roger.

04 47 44   This is Cape, estimating 4 50. Over.

04 47 48   Roger, 04 50

04 47 53   Okay, we're through the peak g now.

04 47 55   Ah, Seven, this is Cape. What's your general condition? Are you feeling pretty well?

04 47 59   My condition is pretty good, but that was a real fireball, boy.

04 48 05   I had great chunks of that retropack breaking off all the way through.

04 48 08   Very good; it did break off, is that correct?

04 48 11   Roger. Altimeter off the peg indicating 80 thousand.

04 48 15   Roger, reading you loud and clear.

04 48 17   Roger.

Asian Longhorned Beetle

The Asian Longhorn Beetle is a prime example of a boring insect. Need we say more? ◉

THE ASIAN LONGHORNED BEETLE and other imported wood boring beetles have been found in wooden crating and packing material associated with trade goods imported from Asia. These beetles are being detected at many ports of entry around the country. Some species are highly destructive, like the Asian Longhorned Beetle, while others are considered of no significance.

For several years, the Asian Longhorn Beetle has been intercepted at points of entry in the United States. Localized infestations were discovered in Illinois (1998) and New York (1996).

Origin:
The native range of the Asian Longhorned Beetle includes Japan, Korea, and China where it is considered a pest of maple, poplar, willow, mulberry, plum, pear, black locust, and elm trees. The Asian Longhorned Beetle is responsible for the destruction of over 400 trees in the Chicago, Illinois, area and has caused an estimated $1.7 million in damage in the Brooklyn and Long Island, New York, area. In New York, the beetle has attacked

species of maple, poplar, willow, and horse chestnut trees. In Chicago, infestations were found in Norway and silver maple, boxelder, elm, and horse chestnut trees.

Description:
The adult beetles are heavy-bodied insects. The approximate length of an adult is 1 1/2 inches. They have a shiny black body with small white markings on their wing covers. They are noted for their long antennae which are banded in black and white and reach way past their bodies.

Symptoms:
Trees with Asian Longhorned Beetle infestations are weakened at first, then die. Damage from this insect and secondary pests will kill a tree within a few years. Dying trees are readily noticeable during the summer months when compared to healthy trees nearby.

Although live specimens of the Asian Longhorned Beetle will be difficult to find outdoors as we enter the winter months, it is possible to see evidence of the beetle such as exit holes in live trees.

Air Bag Safety

If the standard sheep over a fence doesn't put you in a sleepy state, why not imagine SUVs careening into center dividers and deploying their airbags? After reading this selection of airbag wisdom you'll know exactly what drivers need to do to escape bodily harm if they fall asleep at the wheel (even if you can't). ⓥ

Do I need an on-off switch if I buy a vehicle with depowered air bags?

Many manufacturers are installing depowered air bags beginning with their model year 1998 vehicles. They are called "depowered" because they deploy with less force than current air bags. They will reduce the risk of bag-related injuries. However, even with depowered air bags, rear-facing child seats still should never be placed in the front seat and children are still safest in the back seat. Contact your vehicle manufacturer for further information.

Will on-off switches be necessary in the future?

Manufacturers are actively developing so-called "smart" or "advanced" air bags that may be able to tailor deployment based on crash severity, occupant size and position, or seat belt use. These bags should eliminate the risks produced by current air bag designs. It is likely that vehicle manufacturers will introduce some form of advanced air bags over the next few years.

What restraint is right for your child?

WEIGHT OR SIZE OF YOUR CHILD   PROPER TYPE OF RESTRAINT
(Put your child in the back seat, if possible)

Children less than 20 pounds,* or less than 1 year	Rear-facing infant seat *(secured to the vehicle by seat belts)*
Children from about 20 to 40 pounds* and at least 1 year	Forward-facing child seat *(secured to the vehicle by seat belts)*
Children more than 40 pounds*	Booster seat, plus both portions of a lap/shoulder belt *(except only the lap portion is used with some booster seats equipped with front shields)*
Children who meet both criteria below: 1. Their sitting height is high enough so that they can, without the aid of a booster seat, wear the shoulder belt comfortably across their shoulder, and secure the lap belt across their pelvis, and 2. Their legs are long enough to bend over the front of the seat when their backs are against the vehicle seat back	Both portions of a lap/shoulder belt

To determine whether a particular restraint is appropriate for your child, see restraint.

Will following these safety tips guarantee that I will be safe in a crash?

There is no guarantee of safety in a crash, with or without an air bag. However, most of the people killed by air bags would not have been seriously injured if they had followed these safety tips.

Are air bags the reason the back seat is the safest place for children?

No. The back seat has always been safer, even before there were air bags. NHTSA conducted a study of children who died in crashes in the front and back seats of vehicles, very few of which had passenger air bags. The study concluded that placing children in the back reduces the risk of death in a crash by 27 percent, whether or not a child is restrained.

Always secure a rear-facing seat in the back seat. Children age 12 and under should ride in the back seat. While almost all of the children killed by an air bag were 7 years old and younger, a few older children have been killed. Accordingly, age 12 is recommended to provide a margin of safety.

Always wear seat belts. This reduces the distance that they can move forward during a crash. Move the seat toward the rear. The distance between a passenger's chest and the dashboard where the air bag is stored is usually more than 10 inches, even with the passenger seat all the way forward. But more distance is safer.

Buckling Up and Getting Into the Correct Position
How do I stay safe when I'm driving?

Since the risk zone for driver air bags is the first 2-3 inches of inflation, placing yourself 10 inches from your driver air bag provides you with a clear margin of safety. This distance is measured from the center of the steering wheel to your breastbone. If you now sit less than 10 inches away, you can change your driving position in several ways.

- Move your seat to the rear as far as you can while still reaching the pedals comfortably.
- Slightly recline the back of the seat. Although vehicle designs

Deathly Documents

vary, many drivers can achieve the 10-inch distance, even with the driver seat all the way forward, simply by reclining the back of the seat somewhat. If reclining the back of your seat makes it hard to see the road, raise yourself by using a firm, non-slippery cushion, or raise the seat if your vehicle has that feature.

• If your steering wheel is adjustable, tilt it downward. This points the air bag toward your chest instead of your head and neck.

Ingrown Toenails

Here we are back at the feet again. Cardiac research and neuro-science are front-page topics, but do your ingrown toenails get any attention? Not on your life. Read up, treat those toes, and get some rest. ◉

What is an ingrown toenail?
The sides or corners of an ingrown toenail curl down and dig into the skin, causing swelling, pain, and redness.

What causes an ingrown toenail?
While many things can cause ingrown toenails, two major causes are poorly fitting shoes and improperly trimmed nails. Shoes that are too tight press the sides of the nail and encourage it to curl in. Nails that are peeled off at the edge or trimmed down into the corners are also more likely to become ingrown.

To avoid ingrown toenails, nails should be cut straight across.

What is the best treatment for a painful toenail?
When the problem is mild, all you may have to do is soak your foot in warm water and place dry cotton, such as part of a cotton ball, under the corner of the nail. Signs that the problem is getting worse include increasing pain, swelling, and drainage of the

area. Sometimes surgery is needed to remove the outside part of the nail that is poking into the skin.

What kind of surgery is performed to fix the toenail?
Your doctor will first numb your toe by injecting it with an anesthetic. Then your doctor will cut your toenail along the edge that is growing into the skin, and pull out the piece of nail. Finally, your doctor may apply a small electrical charge or liquid solution to the exposed part of the nail bed so that the toenail will not grow into the skin again. This part of the surgery is call ablation, and your doctor will decide whether it needs to be done. Not all patients need ablation.

What should I do to care for my foot after surgery?
1. Soak your foot daily in warm water.
2. Apply antibiotic ointment at least twice a day to the site.
3. Keep a bandage over the site until it heals.
4. Take acetaminophen (Datril, Panadol, Tylenol) or ibuprofen (Advil, Medipren, Motrin, Nuptrin) as needed for pain.
5. Keep the wound clean and dry. It is okay to shower the day after surgery.
6. Wear loosely fitting shoes or sneakers for the first two weeks.
7. Avoid running or strenuous activity for two weeks. Call your doctor if you have problems with the area, such as increasing pain, swelling, redness, or drainage.
8. Avoid high heels and tight-fitting shoes in the future.
9. Trim nails straight across. Don't pick at your nails or tear them at the corners.

Dog Training Tips

If it's that barking dog that's keeping you awake for the fourth straight night, you might take some comfort in learning about what your neighbor hasn't bothered to do. If these tips don't manage to make you drowsy and the barking continues, you might try reading the Tax Preparation Instructions (page 209) to the dog. ⓨ

Barking
Why do dogs bark?
Barking is a natural canine activity. Dogs bark to communicate with you and with others and some bark more than others do. Dogs use different tones of barks to communicate with different things. They may bark in a high-pitched tone which can be associated with greetings, play, fear, or anxiety. A deeper and lower-pitched bark may be a sign of a warning or a threat.

Dogs may bark when they have nothing else to do—they are bored and try to entertain themselves. Some dogs find this to be a good way to burn off some of that energy and some dogs bark simply to hear their own voice—they don't seem to be barking at anything in particular. If a dog feels socially isolated and alone he may react to the isolation by barking. Even if they have a big yard to themselves, they are anxious when left alone, regardless of where they are.

Dogs can also bark because they want or need something. Perhaps they need to eliminate, want to play, or can't find their favorite toy. Other dogs bark for territorial reasons, when other people walk by or other animals are too close to "his" property. Dogs may even bark when they hear something, but don't see it. This can be very annoying to you and especially your neighbors. Sleepless nights will aggravate neighbors who may report the problem to authorities, or can even lead to abuse of the dog. Before barking becomes excessive, you will need to identify the underlying reason for the barking before trying to prevent it or minimize it. Why is the dog barking? Is there a cat or children playing outside? Does he need to eliminate? Is he bored? If the dog is outside and barks because he is bored, then why is he outside? What could you change about the situation?

Solutions

A dog finds his voice as a puppy—where he will like to use it and how to use it. As with all dog behaviors, it is a lot easier to teach your puppy that you will not tolerate excessive barking, rather than wait until he is used to it. Excessive barking does not go away if you ignore it. Since barking is the way dogs communicate, you cannot expect that dogs never bark.

Learn to control your dog's barking. Decide when and how much barking is permissible. If the dog is barking because he is bored, give him something to do. Spend time with him—training, walking, or just playing. Give him plenty of exercise. If you can't be around him all the time, give him some dog and chew toys he likes. If your dog is an outside dog it is time to change that. Bring him inside more often so he can be around you and your family members.

Dogs are social animals and don't want to be separated from their "pack" (which is you). They feel distressed and think they've done something wrong. Let them be a part of the family! If your dog is barking because he is afraid of people or things in his environment, you need to help him to be less afraid. Training classes will help your dog to get more socialized, making sure the experience is pleasant and fun. Invite people over to the house and have them give him a special treat so he will learn that he has nothing to fear from other people.

The worst thing you could do is to give him a treat to "shut him up." What you would be doing is rewarding your dog when he's barking. He will figure this out very quickly: treat when barking—overlooked when quiet. What would you do if you were this dog? If your dog is barking because he sees or hears things, the best thing is to bring him inside. If he is barking at something in the house (some dogs look out of the window to see what's going on) simply block his view. Remove the dog from what is causing him to bark, rather than scolding him. As with all corrections, never call the dog to you to be scolded.

Jumping

Why do dogs jump?

Dogs jump for a lot of reasons. In the wild, wolves greet each other, so they can get face to face. Our dogs do the same thing, but since we are much taller than they are, they have to jump up to greet us face to face. Another reason why dogs jump is that dogs establish rank by body posture. You can see this behavior watching two dogs at play: they are placing their paws on each other's shoulders. In most cases, jumping is a greeting behavior, but for some dogs it means a dominance challenge. Either way, the best time to stop jumping behavior is when the dog is still a puppy. It was cute when he jumped up as a puppy and gave you a big slobber kiss? Well, by now he's probably an adult dog and the jumping behavior is not so cute anymore. Whatever you let your dog do as a puppy, he will do as an adult. So what do you do, since your puppy is now an adult dog and you don't want to tolerate jumping?

Solutions

The easiest solution is to teach your dog how to sit. When he sits, he can't jump; it is physically impossible to do both at the same time. Try preventing the jumping behavior. You need to

Tedious Tips

anticipate when your dog is going to jump—don't wait until he's already airborne! When your dog runs toward you to greet you, have him sit when he gets near you. Then you squat down to your dog's level (remember he was trying to get fact to face with you by jumping) and immediately praise him in a calm voice. Don't make a big deal out of coming and leaving. When you come home, greet your dog warmly, but casually. The less hysterical you are, the less hysterical your dog will be.

If your dog gets excited about going for walks and likes to jump up then, make him sit before you put the leash on. He will quickly learn that if he wants to go for a walk, he needs to sit calmly before you attach his leash. By teaching your dog early on to sit when he greets people, he is less likely to jump. If he does, it is time to teach him the "Off" command. Do not confuse this with the down command. Let's assume your dog jumped up on the couch and you tell him "Down." What do you think your dog will do? He will lay down ON the couch, and that's not what you wanted. You can't get mad at him for doing so, because he did just what you have told him to do.

The "Off" command means that the dog needs to remove himself from whatever he is on. "Off" does not mean that you push, pull, or shove your dog away. In fact, pushing your dog away or down to the ground will trigger more jumping behavior. He will think it is a game—"I jump, you push, then I jump again and you push me again." What a fun game for a dog. Until your dog learns to Sit, use the "Off" command. Watch your dog closely and act quick when he might jump up. If he is in the motion to jump, take a quick step backwards as you sharply give the "Off" command. The dog will have nothing to put his feet on and will fall back to the standing position. Right after the "Off" command, you follow with the "Sit" command. As soon as your dog follows the "Sit" command praise him! This works even better when you have your dog on a leash. Have your foot on the lead (where the leash hits the floor) and he will have no slack to go farther and is corrected by the leash (quickly stomping on the leash and letting your dog's face slam into the floor is NOT acceptable!).

If you are going to teach your dog not to jump on people, it is important that you expose him to people. Locking him into a separate room or leaving him outside isolates him, and he does not have the opportunity to learn to stop jumping. The more people he meets, the more control he will have and, therefore, the less likely he will jump. Have your family members practice with your dog. Children tend to get dogs excited and it is important that your dog learns not to jump on children or elderly people. This can be outright dangerous to them. Be patient and prepared when teaching the dog not to jump.

Do not do any of these things to stop your dog from jumping:

• Stepping on the back paws.
• Hitting the dog in the chest with your knee.
• Holding the dogs front paws until he can't stand anymore.
• Painfully squeezing the dog's front paws.
• Slapping your dog across the front of his nose.

Crate Training

Crate training is probably one of the most misunderstood concepts in training dogs and puppies.

We look at a crate as nothing more than a cold cage that wild animals are kept in. We wouldn't be putting our best friend in a cage, so why would we put our little four-legged buddy in a cage?

Think like a dog for minute. Dogs are pack animals. They live together, hunt together, and play together. They also sleep together, preferably in a cave or a dug out hole in the ground.

This tight "den" (like the crate) give the dogs a sense of security and a place to call "home." This deep-seated den instinct is why family dogs often lie under kitchen tables, underneath beds or closets.

Providing a crate for your dog is one of the best things you can do for him, if you do it correctly and see to it that his social, activity, and play needs are met. It's just like a child's playpen. It keeps your little one out of trouble he's bound to get into if left unsupervised and unconfined. It's also very effective when

Tedious Tips

used in housebreaking and problem-solving, and is the safest and smartest way to transport the dog in your vehicle. And when the family is away, it's the one place your dog will feel secure.

At first, the crate is used to confine your dog for short periods of time during his adjustment stage. The door is kept open so the dog has a safe place to go in and rest, and is closed to keep him from soiling the floor and teething on your furniture. Later it also serves as an indoor dog house, a sanctuary so to speak. Most dogs learn to love their crates because they feel secure in their "den" and use it when they need a place to be alone.

There are several issues to consider when crate training a puppy or dog. Choose the right crate, one that fits your dog's size in order to feel comfortable and secure. The dog should be able to lie down flat, stand up straight, and turn around in the crate. Pet stores will be able to help you chose a crate for your dog.

Sleepercize

Was that great or what?! Now, the quiz:
How do dogs feel when they're left alone?
a. Bored.
b. Anxious
c. Like watching TV.

How can you stop your dog from barking?
a. Give him a tranquilizer
b. Take him shopping.
c. Play with him.

Why do dogs jump?
a. So they can reach the top of the refrigerator.
b. To greet us face to face.
c. To stretch their legs.

When should you use the "Off" Command with your dog?
a. When he is jumping.
b. When you want him to turn off the computer.
c. When you want him to stop licking your face.

Which of these should you not do to get your dog to stop jumping?
a. Discuss it with him calmly.
b. Painfully squeeze his front paws.
c. Take him to therapy.

Tedious Tips

Income Tax Instructions

If you can overcome your sense of dread long enough to read it, these tax filing instructions for the State of Minnesota will bring down the eyelids in a St. Paul minute. Extra credit if you actually manage to figure your tax for this year. Ⓨ

Changes to Forms M-1 and M-1A

Both the M-1 and M-1A have a new line for married couples who file separate returns. In the filing status area there are spaces to enter the name and social security number of your spouse.

Also, if you are using Form M-1 and have part or all of your refund applied to your 1997 estimated tax, you will have one new line to complete. Line 17 now shows your total refund, line 18 the amount you actually want sent to you, and line 19 the amount you want applied to your 1997 estimated tax.

Finally, if you use a professional tax preparer, you can check the new box at the bottom of the form that authorizes us to discuss the return with your preparer.

Where, when, and how to file your return

Due date for filing and paying your tax is April 15. Your 1996 return must be postmarked or brought to the Department of Revenue no later than April 15, 1996.

Mail your Form M-1 or M-1A and all attached Minnesota and federal forms and schedules using the printed envelope in this booklet.

If you don't have the envelope, mail to:

Minnesota Individual Income Tax
St. Paul, MN 55145-0010

Or, take your return to the Department of Revenue's main office at South Robert and Fillmore streets, across the Mississippi River from downtown St. Paul. If you owe a tax, you may pay it there.

Use enough postage! If you enclose more than three sheets of paper, you will probably need additional postage.

File electronically

Filing your state and federal tax returns electronically is as easy as talking to your tax preparer or taking your completed form to an authorized electronic filing transmission site. If you have questions about electronic filing or want the name of an authorized filer near you, call us at (612) 296-8095, or toll-free 1-800-657-3720.

Electronic filing gets you fast filing and verification of your Minnesota return within 24 hours. And refund checks are mailed within 15 days or directly deposited into your bank or credit union account in 10 business days.

Working Family Credit

The Minnesota credit is 15 percent of your federal earned income credit. If you are eligible for the federal earned income credit, you are also eligible for the Minnesota working family credit. This credit is different from the child and dependent care credit, and you may be entitled to both. Claim the working family credit on either Form M-1 or M-1A.

You may be eligible for the working family credit if you:

• lived with a child under age 19 and you earned wages of less than $25,078, or

Deathly Documents

- lived with more than one child under age 19 and you earned wages of less than $28,495, or
- are between 25 and 64, had no dependents, and you earned wages of less than $9,500.

Common mistakes that lead to audits

Every year the Department of Revenue routinely verifies information on your income tax return. Here are common problem areas that cause audits or adjustments:

- Line 1 of your Minnesota return must equal your federal taxable income, even if you were not a full-year Minnesota resident.
- State income tax deducted on your federal return must be added back on line 2 of the Minnesota return. If you itemized deductions on your federal return, you must use Form M-1 and the worksheet on page 8 to determine the line 2 addback amount.
- Income from non-Minnesota municipal bonds is taxable in Minnesota. If you have such income, include it on line 3 of Form M-1.
- Subtractions on line 6 must be clearly identified and properly computed. Please follow the instructions for line 6 of Form M-1 carefully.
- If you have a balance due of $500 or more on line 20, you may owe a penalty. Please see the instructions for line 21 of Form M-1.

Minnesota residents

Any person who was a resident of Minnesota for all of 1996 and who is required to file a 1996 federal income tax return must also file a 1996 Minnesota income tax return.

If you're not required to file a 1996 federal income tax return, you're not required to file a 1996 Minnesota income tax return. However, if your employer withheld Minnesota income tax from your wages in 1996, you must file a Minnesota income tax return if you want a refund of the tax that was withheld.

Members of the Armed Forces
If Minnesota is listed as your legal residence on your service records, you must file a Minnesota income tax return as a resident regardless of where you were stationed in the United States in 1996.

Did you move into or out of Minnesota in 1996?
If you moved into or out of Minnesota in 1996, you must file a Minnesota income tax return if you meet the filing requirements for part-year residents in the section titled Filing requirements for part-year residents and nonresidents.

If you have to file a Minnesota income tax return, you must use form M-1, Minnesota Individual Income Tax Return. Also file Schedule M-1NR, Nonresidents/Part-Year Residents, to determine how much of your income was received when you were a resident of Minnesota and how much of your income came from sources in Minnesota. You'll pay Minnesota tax on that income only. To file, fill in lines 1 through 8 of Form M-1, complete Schedule M-1NR, and continue with line 9 of Form M-1. Be sure to check the box for M-1NR on line 9 of Form M-1.

If you considered Minnesota to be your home permanently or for an indefinite period of time in 1996, you were a resident in 1996.

If you want more information on Minnesota residency requirements, you may request a brochure from the Department of Revenue. Use the order form on the back cover.

Were you a resident of another state and lived in Minnesota?
If you were a resident of another state for all or part of 1996, you may be required to file a Minnesota tax return if both of these conditions applied to you in 1996:

1. you were in Minnesota for 183 or more days during the tax year, and
2. you or your spouse owned, rented, or leased a house, townhouse, condominium, apartment, mobile home, or cabin

Deathly Documents

with cooking and bathing facilities in Minnesota, and it could be lived in year-round.

If both conditions apply to you, you are considered a Minnesota resident for as many days as the second condition applies. If the second condition applied for the entire year, you are considered a Minnesota resident for income tax purposes. If it applied for less than the full year, you are considered a part-year resident and you must file a Minnesota Form M-1 if you meet the filing requirements explained in the next section.

Filing requirements for part-year residents and nonresidents

1. Determine your total income from all sources (including sources not in Minnesota) while you were a Minnesota resident.
2. Determine the total of the following types of income you received while you were a nonresident of Minnesota:
    - wages, salaries, fees, commissions, tips, or bonuses for work done in Minnesota.
    - rents and royalties received from property in Minnesota.
    - gains from the sale of land or other tangible property in Minnesota.
    - gross income from a business or profession conducted partly or entirely in Minnesota. Gross income from a partnership or S corporation is the amount on line 21 of Schedule M-KPI or M-KS. Gross income is income before any deductions or expenses.
    - Gross winnings from gambling in Minnesota.
3. Add the results in steps 1 and 2. If the total is $6,550 or more, you must file Minnesota Form M-1 and Schedule M-1NR. Fill in lines 1 through 8 of Form M-1, complete Schedule M-1NR, and continue with line 9 of form M-1.

If the amount was less than $6,550 and you had amounts withheld or you paid estimated tax, complete the first ten lines of

Schedule M-1NR. Put zero on line 22 of the M-1NR. Check the box for M-1NR on line 9 of Form M-1.

Michigan, North Dakota, and Wisconsin Residents

Minnesota has reciprocity agreements with three neighboring states. If in 1996, you were a resident of Michigan or North Dakota who returned to your home state at least once a month, or were a Wisconsin resident and your only Minnesota income was from the performance of personal services (wages, salaries, tips, commissions, bonuses), you are not subject to Minnesota income tax. However, if Minnesota income tax was withheld from your wages, you must file Minnesota Form M-1 to get a refund. Do not use Form M1-A.

Complete line 1 of your Form M-1 using the appropriate amount from your federal return. Also fill in that amount on line 6 and write reciprocity to the left of line 6. Complete the rest of form M-1. Attach your Minnesota W-2 and a completed Form MW-R, Reciprocity Exemption/Affidavit of Residency, or a completed copy of your home state tax return. Do not complete Schedule M-1NR.

If you're a resident of Wisconsin, Michigan, or North Dakota who works in Minnesota and you want to prevent withholding of Minnesota income tax from your pay in the future, be sure to file a copy of Form MW-R with your employer.

If your gross income assignable to Minnesota from sources other than the performance of personal services is $6,550 or more, you are subject to Minnesota tax. You must file Form M-1 and Schedule M-1NR. Fill in lines 1 through 8 of Form M-1, complete Schedule M-1NR, and continue with line 9 of Form M-1. Check the box for M-1NR on line 9 of Form M-1.

If filing a joint return, and only one person works in Minnesota under a reciprocity agreement, you still must include the names of both spouses and both Social Security numbers on Minnesota Form M-1.

American Indians

If you are an American Indian who lived on a reservation in

Minnesota during all of 1996, you must file Minnesota Form M-1 if:

• you received income from sources outside the reservation, and
• you are required to file a federal income tax return.

If you have to fill out Form M-1 and you are an enrolled tribal member, you may subtract from your federal taxable income any income you received from sources on the reservation while you lived on the reservation. If you subtract reservation income, you must also apportion any working family credit or child care credit you claim. These credits are not allowed on income you received from sources on the reservation while you lived on the reservation.

Due date for filing is April 15
Your 1996 Minnesota income tax return must be postmarked or brought to the Department of Revenue no later than April 15, 1997.

If you file your tax according to a fiscal year, your return must be postmarked or brought to the Department of Revenue no later than the 15th day of the fourth month after the end of your fiscal year.

If you are eligible to receive an income tax refund for 1996, you must file your 1996 return no later than October 15, 2000, to get your refund.

Due date for paying is April 15.

Your tax payment is due in full by April 15, 1997. If you are unable to complete your return by that date and you want to avoid interest and penalties, get Minnesota Form M-13, Payment of Income Tax, from the Department of Revenue. Send in your tax payment using Form M-13 by April 15.

Estimated payments
If Minnesota income tax isn't withheld from your income
If your income includes commissions, dividends, or other

sources not subject to withholding, you must pay Minnesota estimated income tax for 1997 if you expect to owe $500 or more in Minnesota income tax after you subtract:

- the amount of Minnesota income tax you expect to be withheld, if any, from your income for 1997, and
- the amount you expect to receive, if any, for your Minnesota child and dependent care credit for 1997 and the amount you expect to receive for the working family credit for 1997.

You can determine when to make estimated tax payments and how much to pay by reading the instructions for Form M-14, Minnesota Individual Estimated Tax Voucher.

If you receive M-14sc vouchers from the department preprinted with your name and Social Security number, check to make sure the Social Security number(s) is correct. If not, cross out the incorrect number and write in the correct number next to it. It is important that you also cross out the numbers (the scan line) at the bottom of the voucher. Do not make any other changes to the voucher. Instead, use the address card you received with your M-14sc vouchers to make address and any other changes. Preprinted vouchers with the correction will be sent to you next year.

Penalties
Late payment penalty

Your tax is due on the due date of your return—April 15 for most individuals—even if you have an extension to file your federal return. If you file your return by the deadline but you pay your tax after the deadline, you will have to pay a penalty for late payment of tax.

If you are unable to pay the full amount due, pay as much as you can with your return to reduce your penalty and call 1-800-664-3592 for information on payment arrangements.

If you pay your tax 30 days or less after the deadline, the penalty for late payments is 3 percent of the unpaid tax.

If you pay your tax more than 30 days after the deadline, the

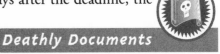

Deathly Documents

penalty for late payment is 3 percent of the unpaid tax plus an additional 3 percent of the unpaid tax for each 30 days or fraction of 30 days that the tax remains unpaid.

The maximum penalty for late payment is 24 percent.

Late filing penalty

There is no late filing penalty as long as your return is filed within six months of the due date. If your return is not filed within six months of the due date, a late filing penalty equal to 10 percent of the unpaid tax will be assessed.

Other penalties

In addition to the penalties listed above, there are also penalties for failing to include all taxable income, and for making an error in determining the amount of tax you owe because you intentionally disregarded the income tax instructions or laws.

Also, there are civil and criminal penalties for intentionally failing to file a Minnesota income tax return and for intentionally filing a false or fraudulent Minnesota income tax return.

Interest on unpaid tax and penalties

You must pay interest on the amount of the penalty as well as on the amount of tax you owe. The interest rate is 8 percent per year. Interest will be assessed from April 15, 1997.

Taxpayer Rights Advocate

If you have tax problems and have had no success in trying to resolve them through normal channels, you may contact the Taxpayer Rights Advocate. Write to:

> Taxpayer Rights Advocate
> Minnesota Department of Revenue
> Mail Station 4000
> St. Paul, MN 55146-4000

Special situations

If the IRS changes or audits your federal tax return . . .
    and if the change or audit affects your Minnesota income tax

return, you have 180 days to file an Amended Minnesota Income Tax Return, Form M-1X, with the Department of Revenue.

If the changes made by the IRS do not affect your Minnesota income tax return, you must, within 180 days, write a letter to the Minnesota Commissioner of Revenue explaining why not. Attach a copy of the report you received from the IRS regarding the changes to your federal tax return.

If you don't file Form M-1X or report the federal changes within 180 days after the IRS notifies you, a penalty will be assessed. The penalty is 10 percent of the amount of underpaid Minnesota tax attributable to the federal change.

Also, if you file an amended federal income tax return, you must send a copy of it to the Minnesota Department of Revenue no later than 180 days after filing the amended federal income tax return.

If a person died before filing

If a person received income in 1996 and died in 1996 or in 1997 before filing a return, a Minnesota income tax return should be filed for the deceased person by his or her spouse or personal representative. The return should be filed using the same filing status as was used to file the final federal income tax return for the deceased person.

If you are filing a Minnesota income tax return for a deceased person, fill in the deceased person's name and your address in the name and address section of the form. Print Deceased and the date of death after the person's name.

If you are claiming a refund on behalf of a deceased person

If you are the decedent's spouse and you are using the joint filing method, the Department of Revenue will send you the refund.

If you are the personal representative, you must attach to the decedent's final income tax return a copy of the court document appointing you as personal representative. You will receive the decedent's refund on behalf of the estate.

If no personal representative has been appointed for the decedent and there is no spouse, you must fill out Form M-23, Claim for a Refund Due a Deceased Taxpayer, and attach it to the decedent's income tax return.

Use your address label

If you received this booklet or a postcard in the mail, take the label from the front and attach it to your form. If you use your label, the Department of Revenue can process your return more accurately and provide more timely service.

If your Social Security number is wrong or any other information is inaccurate, cross out the wrong information and write in the correct information.

If you go to a tax preparer, bring your label to attach when you sign your return.

Information you're not required to provide

Although requested on your Form M-1 and Form M-1A, you are not required to fill in:

- a check in any box for the State Elections Campaign Fund,
- your daytime telephone numbers,
- the telephone number and Minnesota tax ID number orSocial Security number of the person you paid to prepare your return for you.

All other information required

You are required by Minnesota law to provide all other information in order to determine your correct tax liability. If you don't provide it, the Department of Revenue will return your form to you. This will delay your income tax refund, or if you owe tax, your payment will not be processed and you may have to pay a penalty for late payment. Although it is not required, we ask for your daytime telephone number in case we have a question about your return.

Use of information from your income tax return

All information you fill in on your Form M-1 or Form M-1A is private. The Department of Revenue will use the information to determine your tax liability and may, according to state law, share some or all of the information with:

- the IRS and other state governments for tax administration purposes.
- Minnesota state or county agencies to which you owe money.
- another person who must list some or all of your income or expenses on his or her Minnesota income tax return.
- the Minnesota Department of Human Services for purposes of child support collection, the telephone assistance program, the supplemental housing allowance, or the MinnesotaCare program.
- a court that has found you to be delinquent in child support payments.
- the Minnesota Department of Economic Security if you received unemployment compensation.
- the Minnesota Racing Commission if you apply for or hold a license issued by the commission, or own a horse entered in an event licensed by the commission.
- any Minnesota state, county, or city or other local government agency that you are asking to issue or renew your professional license or your license to conduct business, including a gambling equipment distributor licenses and a bingo hall license.
- the Minnesota Department of Labor and Industry for purposes of administering tax and workers' compensation laws.
- the Minnesota Department of Trade and Economic Development if you are participating in an enterprise zone.
- a county, city, or town government that has been designated as an enterprise zone.
- the Minnesota State Lottery before you can contract to sell lottery tickets, or if you win a lottery prize of $600 or more.
- a local assessor for purposes of determining whether homestead benefits have been claimed appropriately.
- the Department of Health for purposes of the MinnesotaCare program and epidemiologic investigation.

- the Legislative Auditor for purposes of auditing the Department of Revenue.
- sources necessary to use statutorily authorized collection tools.
- a district court to determine eligibility for a public defender

If you owe Minnesota or federal taxes . . .

or if you owe criminal fines, a debt to a state or county agency, district court, a municipal hospital, or a public library, state law requires the Department of Revenue to apply your refund to the amount you owe (including penalty and interest on the taxes). If the amount you owe is less than your refund amount, you will receive the difference.

State elections campaign fund

If you want $5 of state money to go to help candidates for state offices pay campaign expenses, check a box for the party of your choice. (If you check the box for the general state campaign fund, the $5 will be distributed among candidates of all parties.) Your spouse may also check a box if you are filing a joint return.

Checking a box will not increase your tax or reduce your refund.

If you think you may be able to file the short form, Form M-1A, see page 6.

Instructions for Form M-1 begin on page 8.

The forgotten tax

Did you know you have to pay Minnesota sales tax when you buy something out of state or out of the country?

It's true, only we give it a different name: use tax. It applies to all things bought through mail order, radio or TV ads, or directly from out-of-state companies.

If you weren't charged sales tax at the time of purchase, you'll have to pay Minnesota's 6.5 percent rate. Otherwise you'll pay the difference between the rate you were charged and Minnesota's rate. In either case, you need for UT-1, Individual Use Tax Return.

The good news is that if your purchases total less than $770, you don't have to file the return.

You can get UT-1 by calling—(612) 296-6181 or 1-800-657-3777, or download the form from our web site—*http://www.taxes.state.mn.us*

UT-1 is due April 15

Sleepercize

If you were an American Indian and made $45,000 in 1999, deducted two children, office space, 17,000 dollars in business expenses, and 480 dollars in out of pocket medical expenses, how much would you owe the government?

Deathly Documents

Halcion Dosage Information

Hey, even if you can't get your hands on the popular sedative Halcion, you can still enjoy the guidelines for dosage. Needless to say, your cough-syrup technique of swigging directly from the bottle is not applicable here. Ⓨ

BENZODIAZEPINES (SLEEP-INDUCING) – ORAL
Uses: This medication is used to treat insomnia (sleeping disorders).

HOW TO USE THIS MEDICATION: Take this medication 15 to 20 minutes before bedtime as directed.

Take this with food or milk if stomach upset occurs.

Do not suddenly stop taking this medication without first consulting your doctor if you have been taking this for some time. It may be necessary to gradually decrease the dose.

Take this exactly as prescribed. Do not increase the dose or take this for longer than prescribed. Tolerance may develop with long term or excessive use making it less effective.

SIDE EFFECTS: Stomach upset, blurred vision, headache, dizziness, depression, impaired coordination, rapid heart rate, trembling, weakness, memory loss, hangover effect (grogginess), clouded thinking, dreaming, or nightmares may occur. If any of these effects continue or become bothersome, inform your doctor.

Notify your doctor if you develop chest pain, rapid heart rate, jaundice, difficulty breathing, skin rash, fever, mental confusion, or seizures while taking this medication.

To avoid dizziness and lightheadedness when rising from a seating or lying position, get up slowly. Also limit your intake of alcoholic beverages which will aggravate these effects.

PRECAUTIONS: Tell your doctor if you have any pre-existing kidney disease, liver disease, a history of drug dependence, depression, breathing problems, apnea, seizures, or if you have any allergies.

This medication should not be used during pregnancy. Discuss the risks and benefits with your doctor. Since small amounts of this medication are found in breast milk, consult your doctor before breast-feeding.

DRUG INTERACTIONS: Tell your doctor of any over-the-counter or prescription medication you may take including any medication for depression or seizures, pain relievers, or sedatives.

NOTES: You may experience sleeping difficulties the first one or two nights after stopping this medication. Be aware of this effect. If the problem continues, contact your doctor.

Elderly persons are usually sensitive to the effects of this medication. Use cautiously.

MISSED DOSE: Take your dose at or near bedtime. If you miss a dose, do not take it if it is near the time for your next dose. Instead, skip the missed dose and resume your usual dosing schedule. Do not "double-up" the dose to catch up.

STORAGE: Store at room temperature between 59 and 86 degrees F (15 to 30 degrees C) away from heat and light. Do not store in the bathroom.

Your Boring Body

Soporific Classics

The Story of the Odyssey

There are some excellent, gripping contemporary translations available of Homer's Odyssey. *Rest assured this is not one of them. If this dreary evocation of the land of the dead doesn't have you fast asleep before the end, try a little of the Descendents of Esau (page 28) as a nightcap.*

CHAPTER XII
The Dwellings of the Dead
(The Tale of Ulysses)

"AFTER THIS WE MADE READY the ship for sailing, and put the black sheep on board, and so departed; and Circé sent a wind from behind that filled the sails; and all the day through our ship passed quickly over the sea.

"And when the sun had set we came to the utmost border of the ocean, where the Cimmerians dwell, being compassed about with mist and cloud. Never doth the Sun behold them, either when he climbs into the heaven, or when he descends therefrom; but darkness surrounds them. Then I bade two of my comrades make ready the sheep for sacrifice; and I myself dug a pit of a cubit every way, and poured in it a drink-offering of honey and milk, and sweet wine, and water, and sprinkled barley upon the drink-offering. Afterwards I took the sheep and slew them, that their blood ran into the trench. And the sons of the dead were gathered to the place,—maidens, and old men who had borne the sorrows of many years, and warriors that had been slain in battle, having their arms covered with blood. All these gathered about the pit with a terrible cry; and I was sore afraid. Then I bade my comrades flay the carcasses of the sheep, and burn them with fire, and pray to the gods of the dead; but I myself sat down by the pit's side, and would not suffer the souls of the dead to come near unto the blood until I had inquired of Teiresias.

"First of all came the soul of my comrade Elpenor. Much did I wonder to see him, and I asked, 'How comest thou hither, Elpenor, to the land of darkness? and how have thy feet outstripped my ship?' Then said Elpenor: 'I fell from the roof of the palace of Circé, not bethinking me of the ladder, and so brake my neck. But now, I pray thee, if thou lovest wife and father and son, forget me not, when thou returnest to the island of Circé, neither leave me without lamentation or burial. Burn me with fire and my arms with me; and make a mound for me by the shore of the sea, that men may hear of me and of my fate in after time. And set up my oar upon my tomb, even the oar which I was wont to ply among my comrades.'

"Then I said to him, 'All this shall be done as thou desirest.'

"And we sat on either side of the trench as we talked, and I held my sword over the blood.

"After him came to me the soul of my mother, whom I had left alive when I sailed to Troy. Sorely I wept to see her, yet suffered her not to come near and drink of the blood till I had inquired of Teiresias. Then came Teiresias, holding a golden sceptre in his hand, and spake, saying: 'Why has thou left the light of day, and come hither to this land of the dead, wherein is no delight? But come, depart from the pit, and take away thy sword, that I may come near and tell thee true.'

"So I thrust my sword into the scabbard; and Teiresias drank of the blood; and when he had drunk, he spake: 'Thou seekest to hear of thy going back to thy home. Know, therefore, that it shall be with peril and toil. For Poseidon will not easily lay aside his wrath against thee, because thou didst take from his dear son, the Cyclops, the sight of his eye. Yet for all this ye may yet come safe to your home, if only thou canst restrain thyself and thy comrades when ye come to the island of the Three Capes, and find there the oxen and sheep of the Sun. If ye let them be and harm them not, then may ye yet return to Ithaca, though it be after grievous toil. But if not, then shall ye perish. And if thou escape thyself, after long time shalt thou return, having lost all thy comrades, and the ship of strangers shall carry thee; and thou shalt find trouble in thy house, even men of violence that will devour thy substance while they seek thy wife in marriage. And when thou shalt have avenged yourself on these, whether it be by craft, or openly with the sword, then take thine oar and travel till thou come into the land of men that know not the sea, and eat not their meat mingled with salt, and have never looked upon ships nor on oars, which are as the wings of ships. And this shall be a clear token to thee, when another traveller, meeting thee in the way, shalt say that thou bearest a winnowing fan upon thy shoulders: then fix thine oar in the ground and do sacrifice to Poseidon, even a sheep, and a bull, and a boar. And afterwards return to thy home, and offer sacrifice of a hundred beasts to all the gods. And death shall come to thee far from the sea, very gentle, and thou shalt die in thy old age, with the people dwelling in peace about thee.'

"To him I made answer: 'So be it, Teiresias. All these things the gods have ordered after their own will. But tell me this. Here I see the soul of my mother that is dead; and she sits near the blood, but regards me not, nor speaks to me. How can she know me, that I am indeed her son?'

"Then said Teiresias: 'Whomsoever of the dead thou shalt suffer to drink of the blood, he will speak to thee; but whomsoever thou sufferest not, he will depart in silence.'

"So I abode in my place; and the soul of my mother came near and drank of the blood. And when she had drunk, she knew her son, and said: 'My son, why hast thou come into the land of darkness, being yet alive? Hast thou not yet returned to thy home?'

"To her I made answer: 'I came hither to inquire of Teiresias of Thebes, and my home have I not seen. Truly trouble hath followed me from the day that I first went with King Agamemnon to the land of Troy. But tell me, how didst thou die? Did a wasting disease slay thee, or did Artemis smite thee with sudden stroke of her arrow? And my father and my son, have they enjoyment of that which is mine, or have others taken it from them? And my wife, is she true to me, or hath she wedded some prince among the Greeks?'

"Then said my mother: 'Thy wife is true, and sits weeping for thee day and night. And thy son hath enjoyment of thy possessions, and hath his due place at the feasts of the people. But thy father cometh no longer to the city, but abideth in the country. Nor hath he any couch for his bed, but in wintertide he sleeps, even as sleep the slaves in the ashes near the fire, and when the summer comes, in the corner of the vineyard upon leaves. Gently doth he sorrow, waiting for thy return, and the burden of old age lies heavy upon him. But as for me, no wasting disease slew me, nor did Artemis smite me with her arrows; but I died of longing for thee, so sorely did I miss thy wisdom and thy love.'

"Then I was fain to lay hold upon the soul of my mother. Thrice I sprang forward, eager to embrace her, and thrice she passed from out my hands, even as passeth a shadow. And when I said, 'How is this, my mother? art thou then but a phantom, that the Queen of the dead hath sent me?' my mother answered me: 'Thus it is with the dead, my son. They have no more any flesh and bones; for these the might of the fire devours; but their souls are even as dreams, flying hither and thither. But do thou return so soon as may be to the light, and tell all that thou hast seen and heard to thy wife.'"

Lotus Software Agreement

For once you can't just click the "I agree" button and get past it. For sheer tranquilizing effect, there's nothing like a good dose of software licensing to immobilize even the most stubborn subject. If you experience frequent screen-freezes and system crashes in your dreams, discontinue use. Ⓨ

IF YOU DO NOT AGREE with these terms and conditions, do not install the software, and return this entire package within 30 days of purchase for a full refund.

You (an entity or a person) may use the software product identified above (the "Software") in the quantity stated above either on a stand-alone computer or on a network, if you meet the following conditions.

Stand-alone Computer Use For All Products except Lotus Organizer and Lotus SmartPics: You must acquire one copy of the Software for each computer on which the Software will be installed. For Lotus SmartSuite, you may not use the applications on more than one computer. The primary user of the computer may also use the Software on a home and/or laptop computer, provided the Software is used on only one computer at a time. For Lotus Organizer and Lotus SmartPics: You must acquire one copy of the Software for each user. However, you are not required to purchase additional copies of Lotus Organizer, Lotus Notes, or cc:Mail if you are using Organizer for the sole purpose of managing calendars assigned to rooms or resources. When you create Lotus Notes IDs or Lotus cc:Mail users for Organizer Scheduling Agents, you are not required to purchase additional copies of Lotus Notes or cc:Mail. You may also use the Software on a home and/or laptop computer.

Shared Network Use: For All Products except Lotus Organizer and Lotus SmartPics: You may use the Software on a network provided you have purchased Software equal to the maximum number of copies in use at any time. For Lotus SmartSuite, using any of the applications other than Organizer or cc:Mail will be considered using the entire SmartSuite. The Software is "in use" on a computer when it is resident in memory (i.e., RAM) or when executable and other files are installed on the hard drive or other storage device. Software which is stored on a server and not resident in memory on that machine is not considered "in use."

Upgrades: If the Software is an upgrade, you are authorized to use the Software only if you are an authorized user of a qualifying product as determined by Lotus. The upgrade replaces the qualifying product.

You may make one (1) archival copy of the Software.

RESTRICTIONS
You may not alter, merge, modify, or adapt the Software in any way including disassembling or decompiling. You may not loan, rent, lease, or license the Software or any copy. However, you may transfer the Software on a permanent basis provided you transfer the Software, the Software Agreement, and all documentation and media, and you do not retain any copies. Any transfer of the Software must include the most recent update and all prior versions. You may not transfer demonstration and evaluation ("D&E") software for commercial purposes.

COPYRIGHT
All intellectual property rights in the Software and use documentation are owned by Lotus or its suppliers and are protected

Deathly Documents

by United States and Canadian copyright laws, other applicable copyright laws, and international treaty provisions. Lotus retains all rights not expressly granted.

ADOBE TYPE MANAGER SOFTWARE

If your Software contains Adobe Type Manager ("ATM") you may install and use ATM software on up to three (3) computers. Outline Fonts: You agree that you will use the Outline Fonts to reproduce and display typefaces solely for your own customary business or personal purposes on: (i) one printer which either contains a PostScript language interpreter or is attached to a central processing unit which utilizes ATM or the Display Postscript System from Adobe and (ii) one or more workstations utilizing ATM. Except as described in this paragraph, the Lotus Software Agreement (including the Limited Warranty and U.S. Government Restricted Rights) will apply to the ATM Software.

LIMITED WARRANTY

For ninety (90) days from your date of purchase, Lotus warrants that: (i) the Software will substantially conform to the applicable user documentation and (ii) that the magnetic media and the user documentation (if any) are free from defects in materials and workmanship. Lotus will, at its option, either refund the amount you paid or provide you with corrected items at no charge provided that the defective item(s) is (are) returned to Lotus within ninety (90) days from the date of purchase. Except as specifically provided herein, Lotus makes no warrant, representation, promise, or guarantee, either express or implied, statutory or otherwise, with respect to the Software, user documentation, or related technical support, including their quality, performance, merchantibility, or fitness for a particular purpose.

The warranty and remedies set forth herein are exclusive and in lieu of all others, oral or written, express or implied. No Lotus dealer, distributor, agent, or employee is authorized to make any modification or addition to this warranty. This warranty gives you specific legal rights, and you may also have other rights which vary from state to state.

LIMITATION OF LIABILITY

Because software is inherently complex and may not be completely free of errors, you are advised to verify your work and to make backup copies. In no event will Lotus be liable for indirect, special, incidental, economic, cover, or consequential damages arising out of the use of or inability to use the Software, user documentation, or related technical support, including, without limitation, damages or costs relating to the loss of profits, business, goodwill, data, or computer programs, even if advised of the possibility of such damages. In no case shall Lotus' liability exceed the amount paid by you for the Software. Some states or provinces do not allow the exclusion or limitation of implied warranties or limitation of liability for incidental or consequential damages, so the above exclusion or limitation may not apply to you.

U.S. GOVERNMENT RESTRICTED RIGHTS

The Software and/or user documentation are provided with restricted and limited rights. Use, duplication, or disclosure by the Government is subject to restrictions as set forth in FAR 52.227-14 (June 1987) Alternate III(g)(e) (June 1987), FAR 52.227-19 (June 1987), or DFARS 52.227-7013 (c)(1)(iii) (June 1988), as applicable. Contractor/Manufacturer is Lotus Development Corporation, 55 Cambridge Parkway, Cambridge, MA 02142.

GENERAL

The export of this product is governed by the U.S. Department of Commerce under its export administration regulations and by Canadian export regulations.

Should you have any questions concerning this Agreement or Lotus' software use policies: in the U.S., write the Inside Sales and Service, Lotus Development Corporation, 55 Cambridge Parkway, Cambridge, MA 02142, or call 1-800-343-5414; in Canada, write to Customer Service, Lotus Development Canada Limited, P.O. Box 679, Scarborough, Ontario M1K 5C5, or call 1-800-465-6887

Deathly Documents

Sleepercize

Read this agreement four times. Now answer these questions:

a. How many days do you have to return the product and receive a full refund?

b. Under what conditions may you transfer the software?

c. In what event is Lotus liable for damage to the software?

d. Where are the headquarters for Lotus software located?

Vowel Matching

When you take something as enjoyable as singing and break it down to a discrete set of technical exercises, it's amazing how mentally mesmerizing it can become. A sterling example is offered here for the purpose of sending you into a blissful state of repose. ⓨ

QUESTION: When does 2 + 2 = 5? Answer: When barbershop harmony is sung correctly, creating harmonic overtones and "expanded sound."

One of the most important factors in the achievement of choral blend and expanded sound is unity of vowel sounds. Vowels are what we sing and sustain, separated by consonants to make words. When we match vowel sounds, we create like harmonics and the sound expands in intensity through reinforcement. In singing, vowels are created through the natural resonance of the human vocal tract. The tongue, lips, and jaws are used to fashion the resonators into their vowel shapes. Some basic rules to follow when forming vowel sounds are:

1. When producing all vowel sounds, the tip of the tongue should be placed gently on the lower gum ridge, with the tip barely touching the base of the lower teeth. This helps

keep the throat open so the vocal chords can vibrate naturally through the resonators (mouth, throat, and sinus cavities).

2. The jaw should be allowed to relax naturally with a swinging down and back motion.
3. The lips should leave the teeth uncovered.
4. Although the mouth must be open wide, it is not how wide it is open but the shape that is most important.

Every vowel can be sung with one of three mouth shapes: round (example—"oh"), square (example—"ih" as in sit), and oblong (example—"ah" as in pop). Refinements to form each specific vowel sound are made by the degree to which the tongue is arched in the mouth, and the degree to which the jaw is dropped. For instance, both the "oh" sound and the "oo" (as in moor) sound are made with the round mouth shape, but the "oh" sound is made with the mouth as open as possible while the "oo" sound is made with the smallest, most rounded shape.

As we sing the songs in our repertoire, keep in mind the basic mechanics of producing vowel sounds and think about the target vowel sound for each word in the song. Properly matched vowels can enable our chorus of 20-something men to "fill the hall" and create the expanded sound that makes barbershop harmony so much fun to sing and hear.

Sleepercize

Think of every word you can starting with the letters a, e, i, o, and u.

The Battle of Fort Stephenson

History buffs may find this passage utterly absorbing. Anyone else is bound to find this carefully selected bit of obscurity almost as effective as three swigs of Nyquil.

THE FOLLOWING STORY takes place during the War of 1812. The defense of Fort Stephenson by 21-year-old Major George Croghan with his garrison of approximately 160 men—and one cannon—against General Proctor's far superior forces, and his Indian allies, is one of the most amazing victories any war has ever known.

The following story is from the book Historical Sketches of Fremont & Sandusky County

At the onset of the War of 1812 the Northwest was woefully unprepared for the hostilities soon to come. The British in Canada were better prepared, although there were only 4500 troops in Canada at the beginning of the war. However they had trained leadership in Issac Brock, the governor of Upper Canada, and they were prepared to make the best of what they had.

After the declaration of war, June 18, 1812, America's weaknesses became very apparent. On July 17, Fort Mackinac was taken by the British with out a shot being fired. The British seemed to have better communication; consider the fact that on the morning of July 17 the American commander was surprised to find his garrison completely surrounded by 600-700 British and Indians from nearby Fort St. Joseph. The Americans were not informed war had been declared. Obviously, the British were well aware.

Next, the British set their sights on Fort Dearborn. Captain Heald, the commander of the fort, received orders from General William Hull to evacuate the fort, destroy extra arms and ammunition, distribute the extra provisions among the friendly Indians, and burn the fort. For some unknown reason, there was a six day delay in carrying out Hull's orders. This delay gave the Indians enough time to amass great numbers. Just a few miles from the burning fort, the unsuspecting garrison was attacked by Indians. The entire American force was either killed or captured. Of those captured, many were tortured to death. Only 18 soldiers and most of the women were later returned to the Americans.

Further east, General Hull was having difficulties with the Ohio Militia as well. He was proceeding northward from Dayton, with the objective of crossing the Detroit River into Canada and securing Fort Malden. Due to the presence of British men-of-war in the Detroit River, Hull could not take the easily traversed route along the lake, but was forced to take a much more difficult path through the swamps.

While Hull's forces were trudging through the swamps, the British had captured a schooner en route to meet Hull in Detroit. Hull's problems were compounding by the minute and he wasn't even aware of it. The captured schooner was carrying supplies and the muster rolls of Hull's army. Armed with information as to the size of Hull's forces, the British busied themselves reinforcing Fort Malden. News of the reinforced Fort Malden did reach Hull before he got there. This news concerned Hull enough that he withdrew his plans and headed for Detroit. With the control of the Detroit River, the British were able to invade Michigan south of Detroit and cut off Hull's supply lines. Besieged by the British and their Indian allies, Hull was forced to surrender on August 16.

Meanwhile, a general from the west, General Winchester,

led a campaign to chase the Indians, who had taken over Fort Wayne, back to the woods. Also participating in this campaign was Major George Croghan.

At this time plans were being made to combine the forces of General Winchester, General Harrison, and General Tupper at the foot of the rapids of the Maumee River. All three armies, totaling 10,000 troops, were to march on to Detroit, with the objective of taking Detroit by Christmas.

The first leg of the journey General Winchester's troops stopped at the old Fort Defiance. They rebuilt the fort and replenished the supplies. Then, firmly believing that Detroit could be taken by Christmas, General Winchester pressed on, leaving Major Croghan in charge of a small garrison at the newly named Fort Winchester.

It was early November when Winchester and his troops left the fort. Late fall rains and early winter snow fall made the trip slow and strenuous. Despite the fact his men were in poor condition, due to the long winter trudge, and General Harrison's troops had not yet arrived, Winchester continued on toward Detroit. He was hoping to capture Fort Malden with a quick move across the ice on the Detroit River, while the British fleet was immobilized.

A forward attachment of Winchester's troops arrived at Frenchtown on the River Raisin, January 17, 1813. Five hundred fifty men encountered the British and Indians, and defeated them. Three nights later, Winchester and 250 more men arrived in Frenchtown. Still, Winchester's defenses were not near enough to hold back a British attack. However, for some reason, probably because he was expecting reinforcements from General Harrison, Winchester did nothing to bolster his position. This proved to be a costly mistake.

During the night of January 21, a British and Indian army under the direction of General Henry Proctor crossed the ice from Fort Malden and surprised the Americans with an attack at daybreak. Unprepared and attacked by a superior force, a full nine-tenths of Winchester's army was either killed or captured. With the defeat of Winchester, General Harrison withdrew his troops to the more secure regions of the Portage River about 18 miles east of the Maumee River. All of the American fortifications north of the Maumee were destroyed.

Early in February of 1813, American engineers began the construction of a new fort, Fort Meigs. The Americans were well aware of the fact a British attack on this area was inevitable, and they were going to be prepared.

As anticipated, on April 28, 1813, General Proctor and his troops laid siege on the new Fort Meigs. After days and nights of constant bombardment with virtually no effect, Proctor realized the new fort was too strong to be taken by assault, so he withdrew his attack. Another factor leading to Proctor's withdrawal was the arrival of American reinforcements under Brigadier General Green Clay and Lieutenant Colonel William Dudley. They temporarily detained the British on the west bank of the river. However Dudley's forces were mostly killed and captured by the Indians. The Indians were eager to show off their captives and booty, so they returned to their villages. The loss of Indian support and the seemingly impervious Fort Meigs were both factors in Proctor's decision to withdraw.

Proctor's next plan was to attack Presqué Isle, where the Americans were building a fleet necessary to seek control of the lakes. However, after witnessing the unreliability of the Indians, he decided instead to launch an offensive up the Sandusky River. The Indians disagreed with this plan; they wanted to try to take Fort Meigs again. Proctor didn't want to lose his Indian allies. So, reluctantly, he agreed with their plan to attack Fort Meigs. It's possible he thought that with more Indian support, he might be able to take the fort this time. The Indian's plan was to try to trick the Americans into coming out of the fort. It was an ill conceived plan, and of course met with utter failure. General Proctor's concern now, after two unsuccessful campaigns, was the loss of any further Indian support.

Intelligence reports told Proctor Fort Stephenson was weakly constructed and undermanned. Proctor was hoping a campaign against the fort would be just what he needed to impress the Indians, and regain their support. General Proctor gave the order to advance to the Sandusky River shore and launch an attack against Fort Stephenson.

In the late afternoon of August 1, 1813, Proctor's forces appeared at Fort Stephenson. Proctor soon realized his intelligence reports were accurate. The fort consisted of a rectangular picket stockade with two blockhouses: one at the southwest corner, and at the northwest corner, with one in the center of the north wall. Inside were only 160 regulars, mostly Kentuckians, of the newly formed 17th Infantry Regiment. And the fact that the fort was commanded by 21-year-old, Major George Croghan, gave Proctor all the information necessary for him to believe an easy victory was at hand.

General Proctor sent Colonel Matthew Elliot and Captain Peter Chambers to demand Croghan's surrender. Major Croghan sent junior officer Lieutenant Edmund Shipp with the message that they would defend the fort to the last man. The British officers pleaded with Shipp saying, "For God's sake sir, surrender and prevent the dreadful massacre that will be caused by your resistance." Shipp replied, "We will not surrender as long as a man can fire a gun!" As the men were parting company an Indian who was with the British officers jumped Shipp and was apparently trying to grab his sword. The British officers stepped in and prevented the attack. Meanwhile, Major Croghan was heard yelling, "Come in Shipp and we'll blow them all to hell!" Shipp returned to the fort and the stage was set for one of the most amazing battles in history.

Proctor's forces replied to the American's stubbornness with harassing fire that continued through most of the night. Croghan and his men countered with musket fire and shots fired from "Old Betsy." Croghan wanted the British to think he had more artillery than just one old cannon left over from the Revolutionary War, so he had the cannon shifted around the fort after each shot. Most of the British fire was directed toward the northwest corner of the fort. Seeing this, Croghan believed the main attack would come from this angle. Major Croghan directed his men to place Old Betsy in the blockhouse, so that it would spray its fire into that portion of the ditch. By dawn Proctor had three cannons within 250 yards of the northwest corner of the fort. Proctor opened fire with the three six-pounders, again directing all of his fire toward the northwest corner. Now Croghan knew he was right: an assault would have to come from that direction. The fire from Proctor continued all morning and into the afternoon with no effect on the garrison inside. Croghan ordered his men to fire their muskets sparingly to show spirit and trick the British into thinking their fire was taking its toll.

Meanwhile, the Indians, who had agreed to attack the south wall when the British attacked the north, decided on an early retreat into a nearby woods where they remained as spectators for the rest of the battle. Frontal assaults in the face of cannon fire was not an Indian style of fighting.

Soon Proctor was convinced the fire had taken its toll on the small garrison at Fort Stephenson. Proctor now put the final piece of his plan into action. He sent a few men under the direction of Lieutenant-Colonel Augustus Warburton in a wide circle around the fort as a means of deception. Meanwhile, he ordered Lieutenant-Colonel William Shortt and Lieutenant J. G. Gordon to lead the main force in an attack of the north wall. Using the smoke generated from all of the cannonade, the British made their advance on Fort Stephenson. The British made it to within 15–20 yards of the palisades when they were discovered. The Kentucky sharpshooters let loose with a volley of musket balls that sent the British reeling. The British quickly re-grouped and stormed the fort again. Lieutenant Shortt was at the forefront of the party and he was heard to say "Cut away at the pickets, my brave boys, and give the damned Yankees no quarter!" Now it was time for Old Betsy to make herself known. Croghan gave the order, "Now boys, let her speak now!" With that, Old Betsy erupted and left many British dead and injured in her wake. The British made a second attempt, but by now Old Betsy had been recharged; the cannon erupted the second time and had the same effect as the first. Brevet Lieutenant Colonel Shortt and Lieutenant Gordon were both killed in the attack. According to careful estimates, the total loss of British men both killed and wounded was 120. Warburton and his approximately 200 grenadiers did not reach the south side of the fort until after the disaster at the north wall. They were met with a volley of musket balls from Captain Hunter and the men under his command. They were forced to flee and seek shelter in a nearby woods. The entire loss of the American defenders of Fort Stephenson was a mere one man killed and seven only slightly wounded.

What Proctor thought was to be an easy victory turned out to be a bitter and embarrassing loss. The defeat of the British at Fort Stephenson proved damaging to their future strength. Prior to this they had full support of the Indians. With the Fort Stephenson disaster and the two prior losses at Fort Meigs, their ties with the Indians were broken. Further effects of the victory were both immediate and apparent in the Northwest. With the British offensive stymied, Harrison was able to prepare for an American offensive, which he later did quite successfully. In September, Perry defeated the British at Put-in-Bay. Later that month Proctor withdrew from Detroit, the Indians were talking about peace, and Harrison carried the war into Upper Canada, ending forever any real threat to the Northwest. A small garrison led by a resourceful, intelligent young Major provided the strength to turn the tide of the war. Major George Croghan and his men are true heroes of the War of 1812.

Great (Dull) Moments in History

Airline Ticket Fine Print

Who would have guessed that the secret to a sound sleep could be found on the back of the common airline ticket? As you slip into blissful slumber while reading this selection, imagine yourself jetting off to a tranquil tropical paradise, while your luggage wings its way to Des Moines. ⓨ

Advice to International Passengers on Limitation of Liability
Passengers on a journey involving an ultimate destination or a stop in a country other than the country of origin are advised that the provisions of a treaty known as the Warsaw Convention may be applicable to the entire journey, including any portion entirely within the country of origin or destination. For such passengers on a journey to, from, or with an agreed stopping place in the United States of America, the Convention and special contracts of carriage embodied in applicable tariffs provide that the liability of certain carriers, parties to such special contracts, for death of or personal injury to passengers is limited in most cases to proven damages not to exceed U.S. $75,000 per passenger, and that this liability up to such limit shall not depend on negligence on the part of the carrier. The limit of liability of U.S. $75,000 above is inclusive of legal fees and costs except that in the case of a claim brought in a state where provision is made

for separate award of legal fees and costs, the limit shall be the sum of U.S. $58,000 exclusive of legal fees and costs. For such passengers traveling by a carrier not a party to such special contracts or on a journey not to, from, or having an agreed stopping place in the United States of America, liability of the carrier for death or personal injury to passengers is limited in most cases to approximately U.S. $10,000 or U.S. $20,000.

The names of carriers, parties to such special contracts, are available at all ticket offices of such carriers and may be examined on request. Additional protection can usually be obtained by purchasing insurance from a private company. Such insurance is not affected by any limitation of the carrier's liability under the Warsaw Convention or such special contracts of carriage. For further information please consult your airline or insurance company representative.

Notice of Baggage Liability Limitations
Liability for loss, delay, or damage to baggage is limited unless a higher value is declared in advance and additional charges are paid. For most international travel (including domestic portions of international journeys) the liability limit is approximately $9.07 per pound for checked baggage and $400 per passenger for unchecked baggage. For travel wholly between U.S. points federal rules require any limit on an airline's baggage liability to be at least $1250 per passenger. Excess valuation may be declared on certain types of articles. Some carriers assume no liability for fragile, valuable, or perishable articles. Further information may be obtained from the carrier.

Carrier reserves the right to refuse carriage to any person who has acquired a ticket in violation of applicable law or carrier's tariffs, rules, or regulations.

Notice—Overbooking of Flights
Airline flights may be overbooked, and there is a slight chance that a seat will not be available on a flight for which a person has a confirmed reservation. If the flight is overbooked, no one will be denied a seat until airline personnel first ask for vol-

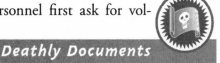

Deathly Documents

unteers willing to give up their reservation in exchange for a payment of the airline's choosing. If there are not enough volunteers the airline will deny boarding to the other persons in accordance with its particular boarding priority. With few exceptions persons denied boarding involuntarily are entitled to compensation. The complete rules for the payment of compensation and each airline's boarding priorities are available at all airport ticket counters and boarding locations. Some airlines do not apply these consumer protections to travel from some foreign countries, although other consumer protections may be available. Check with the airline or your travel agent.

Reconfirmation Notice
Some international carriers require reconfirmation of your reservations. Contact the transporting air carrier for the applicable requirements.

Sleepercize
Close your eyes and count every place you've ever flown on an airplane. Recall each flight in detail. Who did you sit next to? What did you eat? Now, recall every airport you've been in. Count each time, even if you've been in the Detroit airport seventeen times.

Milk Substitutes

Is that glass of warm milk at bedtime doing you more harm than good? Say, perhaps it's lactose intolerance that's keeping you awake! Learn about various milk substitutes and drift off to dreamland at one and the same time. Just be sure to put your glass down first. ⓨ

Soy Milk
Soy milk is made from soybeans and must be fortified with calcium in order to be nutritionally equal to cow's milk. It can be used in cooking in place of milk. The following are lactose-free products:

Eden Foods:	Eden Soy: vanilla, original, and carob
Health Valley:	Soy Moo
Pacific Foods:	Organic Soy Beverage
Soyamel	
Vita Soy Inc.:	Natural Soy Drink, Carob Supreme
WestBrae:	West Soy: vanilla malted, cocoa-mint malted
	West Soy Lite: plain, vanilla, cocoa
	West Soy Plus (calcium added)

Coconut Milk
Some coconut milk may be cow's milk flavored with coconut. The following are lactose-free products:

Andre Prost Inc.:	coconut milk (canned)
JFC:	coconut milk (canned)
Port Arthur:	coconut milk (canned)

Rice Beverages
Rice beverages are made from rice and contain less protein and calcium than milk or dairy products. They are generally lactose free.

Imagine Foods:	Rice Dream

Lactose Intolerance
Lactose intolerance is the inability to digest lactose (milk sugar). The cause of lactose intolerance is a shortage of or lack of the enzyme LACTASE which is normally made by the body in the small intestine. Lactase breaks down milk sugar so that it can be used by the body as energy.

Lactose intolerance is not the same as a "milk allergy." Some people have an allergy to one or more of the proteins in milk, and must avoid milk and milk products. The proteins in milk are: casein, lactoglobulin, and lactalbumin.

People with lactose intolerance can often tolerate a small amount of lactose. This information sheet is provided to help customers in choosing products that are lactose free or that have a reduced lactose content. It is not intended to be a diet information sheet. Consult your physician or dietitian for your individual needs.

Frozen yogurt containing lactose is not as well tolerated as non-frozen yogurt. However, as with milk, small amounts may be tolerated by less sensitive people.

Creamers and Toppings

Lactose Free

FROZEN:

Kraft General Foods:	Cool Whip, Cool Whip Lite
Kemps:	Coffee Creamer
Rich's:	Coffee Rich, Poly Rich, Rich Whip

REFRIGERATED:

Beatrice:	Reddi-wip
Rich's:	Rich Whip
Nestlé:	Carnation Coffee-mate, Coffee-mate Lite,
International Delight:	Non-Dairy Creamer, Amaretto & Irish Cream

DRY/POWDERED:

Beatrice/Hunt-Wesson:	NoRICH
Borden:	Cremora, Cremora Lite
Carnation:	Coffee-mate, Coffee-mate Lite
Preferred Products Inc:	Shoppers Value Non-Dairy Creamer

Frozen Desserts

Lactose Free

Water ices, fruit ices, Italian ices, sorbets, and frozen tofu-based desserts are often lactose free.

Blue Bunny:	Citrus Lites
Dole:	Fruit'n Juice, Fruit Sorbet
Dole Whip:	Low-Fat & Non-Fat Soft Serve
Kemps:	Twin Pops, LITE Pops, Juice Koolers
Luigi's:	Italian Ice
Mama Tish's:	Sorbetto
Mocha Mix:	Non-Dairy Frozen Dessert
Popsicle:	Ice Pops
Rice Dream:	Frozen Non-Dairy Dessert
Savino:	Italian Sorbet
Tofutti:	Non-Dairy Dessert, Tofutti Cuties
Welch's:	Fruit Juices, Juice Bars, no sugar added

Your Boring Body

Sleepercize

Think of every possible food product containing soy. I'll give you a head start: tofu, miso soup, tofutti, tofu-burgers.

Beets

It's come to this: Beets! You've kept your distance at the salad bar; now learn other preparations in which to avoid them.

BEETS WERE ORIGINALLY GROWN for their leaves, but historians tell us that the early Romans ate only the tops, reserving the roots for medicinal purposes. Today table beets are grown commercially in 31 states for both their earthy-sweet roots and their leafy tops.

Selecting beets
Available year-round with the peak season from June through October, the most common color for bunch or table beets is garnet red. Firm, smooth-skinned, small to medium beets are the most tender, as many large beets tend to be woody and strong flavored. Leaves should be green, fresh, and crisp looking.

Storage
To store beets, cut off the green tops leaving 1-2" of stem attached, reserving the beet greens. Do not trim the roots. Refrigerate, unwashed, in a plastic bag for up to 3 weeks. Wash beet greens and pat dry; place in a paper towel-lined plastic bag and refrigerate up to 3 days.

Preparation

Beets are one of the simplest vegetables to prepare. Scrub well, but do not peel. Leave roots, stems, and skin intact to prevent bleeding during cooking. Adding a small amount of lemon juice to the water can minimize color leaching. Let cooked beets cool; trim roots and stems and slip off skins under cold running water. Cooking time for beets varies, depending on their size. Bake, boil, steam, or microwave beets.

Baking: Wrap beets in foil; place on baking sheet. Bake in a preheated 400° oven until tender when pierced with a fork (about 1 hr.), cool.

Boiling: Boil beets, covered in water, until tender (20-45 min.), drain.

Beet greens can be delicious! They are highly nutritious and taste like zesty spinach. Remove leaves from stems, cut the greens into thin strips, and sauté or steam briefly.

Nutritional Highlights

Beets are a good source of vitamin C, potassium, and a fair source of vitamin A. A one cup serving of cooked, diced beets has about 55 calories.

Serving

Try the following serving ideas for cooked beets:

- Top hot sliced beets with butter, salt, pepper, shallots, or a dash of wine vinegar and sprinkle with chives, dill weed, or thyme.
- Thinly slice uncooked beets; pan-fry with sliced onions and season.
- Toss sliced beets in vinaigrette dressing; garnish with parsley.
- Use shredded raw beets in salads or salsa for texture interest.

Dual Currency Economics

If the Tax Preparation Instructions left you wide-awake and frustrated, this interminable lecture on the theory of dual currency systems will tuck you in in a hurry. They don't call it the "dismal science" for nothing!

> *To give us a functioning economic theory, we thus need a new synthesis that simplifies—but so far there is no sign of it. And if no such synthesis emerges, we may be at the end of economic theory.*
> —Peter Drucker, *The New Realities*

WITHOUT A DOUBT, society is moving towards a cashless or paperless economy. Yet old and familiar habits often die hard, and the shift from paper currency and checks to electronic banking and commerce remains a gradual one.

There are certainly many advantages to electronic commerce for consumers and merchants alike. For consumers, there is the safety and security of not carrying cash. There is convenience in not running for cash or not recording every transaction into a check register. There is even a financial advantage from the grace period for those who buy with credit cards. For merchants, there is the convenience and time savings of electronically recorded transactions with no need to count and recount or deposit and record cash and checks. As well, a lower rate of loss from bad or stolen checks saves money for retailers, ultimately providing consumers with lower prices. There are indeed concerns over privacy, but many people also recognize an opportunity to reduce crime, illegal drug sales, welfare fraud, and so forth. On the whole advantages seem to outweigh disadvantages and risks. Yet, to date, significant numbers of people have been unwilling or financially unqualified to make the switch to electronic commerce.

What could be a powerful incentive to speed the transition towards a cashless and paperless banking and transaction system? What about the introduction of a new currency—a currency only available through plastic bank cards—that offered new purchasing power for consumers, new profits for businesses, and new economic development resources for communities? What is the logic behind such a financial innovation? What might be the entrepreneurial opportunities for those with the vision and the skills to be pioneers in its development?

Is it possible that we have outgrown the dollar, and if so, how could we tell? That is actually a fairly simple question. If we look, businesses everywhere seek to sell more of the very goods and services that consumers seek to buy. Only money is missing to allow these transactions to take place. Strangely, money was invented to promote commerce not to inhibit it . . . which raises the issue of re-inventing money.

Re-Inventing Money throughout History

From time to time, innovations in money emerge which improve upon earlier financial tools. These new forms of money appear for two simple and logical reasons—the old money begins to inhibit the growth of commerce, while new technologies make more efficient forms of money both practical and timely.

So it was that the invention of metal smelting led to minting gold and silver coins, which moved commerce beyond the limitations of barter. In a like manner, the invention of printing led to paper currency, which expanded commerce beyond the limitations of gold coins. More recently, the invention of computers and telecommunications systems is elevating commerce light-years beyond the limitations of paper transactions and manual accounting systems.

Is it possible that our current financial instrument—the dollar—could be imposing restrictions upon commerce, despite the vast power and scope of electronic banking? If this were indeed the case, it would be important to speculate on the next generation of money . . . keeping in mind what new technologies now make possible that was not possible even a few short decades ago.

More Goods and Services than Money
Consider the wide array of industries where capacity exceeds consumer purchasing power:

- Most restaurants seek additional customers, while families desire to dine out more often.
- Many auto dealerships have large inventories of high quality new and used vehicles, while numerous individuals desire newer, better, and safer automobiles. At the same time, many auto manufacturers operate well below full capacity.
- Retail stores, department stores, discount stores, and mail order catalogues often have large inventories to sell, while suppliers appeal for orders to fill. Movies, concerts, sports events, and theater performances often have empty seats. Consumers desire more of these products and amusements.
- Numerous colleges and universities are cutting back programs and faculties, even as many individuals, young and old, long for higher education and businesses seek better educated workers.
- Airlines, hotels and motels, resorts, and rental car agencies often operate at partial capacity, yet large numbers of people wish to travel and vacation more.
- Many contractors could readily expand their businesses to build additional quality housing or improve the infrastructure of communities. Meanwhile countless families suffer

from lack of quality housing and communities suffer from deteriorating infrastructure.

In every case, the purchasing power of consumers is not keeping up with the productivity gains and productive capacities of businesses.

A number of questions arise: Why would money or purchasing power for consumers be in short supply, even when products and services are plentiful? Why doesn't an increase in the money supply by the Federal Reserve or an increase in consumer credit narrow the gap between business capacity and consumer demand? In the larger scheme, why doesn't consumer purchasing power automatically advance with improvements in technology and business productivity? Why are wage increases seen as the cause of inflation or a threat to business competitiveness, rather than as a source of prosperity? Lastly, are there other ways for businesses and consumers to engage in commerce when dollars are insufficient?

While some of these questions lie beyond the scope of this article, together they indicate that a re-examination of our economic theories and business practices may be in order. Perhaps a high-tech, information economy—using ever less materials, energy, labor, and capital to produce and distribute ever more goods and services—requires new tools and different rules than an economy based upon scarce material resources?

Excess Business Capacity and the Entrepreneurial Opportunity
To understand why consumer purchasing power consistently lags behind the productivity gains of business, we can begin by observing a common, everyday dynamic in the market.

It is generally agreed that there are many benefits to economic competition. Competition rewards risk-taking, innovation, and hard work. It also contributes to new product development, quality improvement, and better customer service. Particularly at the onset of a new industry or a new product cycle, additional jobs are created and more goods and services become available to consumers.

As more and more companies enter a growing market, what is at first apparent are the economic advantages—growing consumer choice, falling prices, and job creation. As industries mature and once innovative products are copied, there comes a point at which many businesses may offer the same or similar products. Suddenly, the drawbacks of competition begin to rival the benefits—lay-offs, wage stagnation, and, sometimes, whole communities in decline. Yet we are confronted with a strange dilemma or anomaly. While the productive capacity of an industry may be at an all time high, and while there may still be extensive unmet demand for every company's products and services—demand both in the U.S. markets and around the world—consumers lack the purchasing power to acquire these products and services.

The problem points to the entrepreneurial opportunity

Looked at another way, in the battle between companies for sales and market share, consumers certainly benefit from the competition. Yet, proliferation of duplication, falling prices, and declining market shares also put extreme downward pressure on business profits and on the wages that employers can pay to employees. Since employees wages are the single most important source of consumer purchasing power, then downward pressure on wages translates directly into restrictions on consumer purchasing power. These restrictions on purchasing power occur despite any and all advances in technology, improvements in business productivity, growth by various industries, or fiscal and monetary policies by banks and the government. Instead, wage levels primarily reflect the amount of competition in the market.

Fortunately, this very problem points to an entrepreneurial solution and a business opportunity. Competition and duplication—before the onset of downsizing and business consolidations—leads to the sizable growth of underutilized or excess business capacity. Why couldn't a supplemental currency capture and distribute this excess business capacity, creating a new economic resource for businesses, employees, and communities alike. If the new currency was combined with cash, then merchants could cover their cash costs, make an additional incremental cash profit, and still offer consumers a significant portion of the product price in the noncash currency. Under the rules of a cooperative business network, the new currency could be kept in balance with available goods and services, thus avoiding the pitfalls of both inflation and recession.

Introducing dc-commerce and Business Incentive Dollars

If your only tool is a hammer, every problem looks like a nail.
—Abraham Maslow

A novel application of banking and transaction technologies has been designed to address this anomaly in modern economics and to bridge the gap between underutilized business capacity and the limited financial resources of many consumers and communities. The new form of exchange is called dual currency commerce (dc-commerce). The simple premise behind dc-commerce is that cash resources can be stretched or supplemented—without causing inflation—through the use of a noncash, companion currency. As the name suggests, dual currency transactions are priced and settled in two currencies simultaneously. For example, a $10.00 restaurant meal might cost $5.00 cash and $5.00 in a second currency, while a $40.00 pair of pants might cost $34.00 cash and $6.00 in a second currency. In theory, the second currency can help to expand trade and commerce, much the way that paper currency initially augmented gold coins.

Business Incentive Dollars™ (B$) are one example of such a companion currency. B$ are a virtual corporate discount scrip, engineered by blending the best features of U.S. dollars, discounts, barter dollars, corporate scrip, and service credits. While most people are familiar with U.S. dollars and discounts, the other currencies may call for some explanation. Barter dollars or trade credits are a substitute for cash that allow businesses or individuals to exchange with one another when cash is in short supply. Corporate scrip, such as frequent flyer miles, is a privately issued business currency used primarily as a marketing tool in customer loyalty programs. Service credits are a little known community economic development tool that help individuals to trade services with one another on an egalitarian, hour for hour basis.

Technologically simple, dual currency commerce represents an enhancement to existing credit cards, debit cards, smart cards, or EBT cards (Electronic Benefit Transfer cards for government recipients of cash and food stamp benefits). Enhancements are improvements to existing products and services in the transaction industry. This means that with little modification and expense, transaction companies and banks can turn the very cards that consumers now use for spending into earning cards as well. The system also utilizes standard retail point of sale (POS) terminals. Consequently, dual currency commerce can eliminate the inconvenience to merchants and customers of cash, checks, discount coupons, and proprietary point programs. In addition, dc-commerce can be easily applied to e-commerce on the Internet.

There will presumably be a variety of ways to introduce Business Incentive Dollars into operation, including employee incentives, wage subsidies, social security supplements, investor dividends, volunteer rewards, charitable gifts, foundation grants, or tax rebates. Just as with early generations of bank computers or networking software, the first applications of dual currency commerce may appear primitive by later standards. Laws and regulations governing dc-commerce will most likely be designed over time by industry representatives, regulatory agencies, and federal lawmakers—much like the laws and regulation that today govern banking, credit cards, insurance, investing, e-commerce, and other financial industries.

A Sample Transaction

Imagine yourself as a restaurant owner. You first must determine an acceptable ratio of cash to Business Incentive Dollars, as well as any limitations on the times when you will accept B$ or whether discounted specials will be excluded. This is very similar

Deathly Documents

to the rules for "2 for 1" dining coupons or senior citizens discounts. A representative of your dual currency business alliance would help you to design a promotional campaign aimed at its members. There would also be an orientation for your employees. Right from the start, you could enjoy an influx of new customers and a modest, incremental cash profit with each sale. You would receive dual currency statements from your transaction processor—such as Visa or MasterCard—and your employees would receive dual currency bank statements from their banks.

You and your employees now earn B$ on top of cash. Cash revenues are still distributed in the traditional way towards materials, labor, overhead, and profit. Business Incentive Dollars might be distributed as dividends from the dual currency business alliance (dcba). In your dcba, every person, whether employee, manager, or owner, might receive an equal dividend of B$350.00 per month, prorated for a 40 hour work week. Employees, who were earning $8.00 per hour, would now earn an extra B$2.00 per hour for a total of $10.00 per hour in effective purchasing power. Such across the board raises increases everyone's purchasing power some, but they make the biggest difference for those at the bottom of the economic ladder.

When you and your employees go to spend your B$, here is what you find: an evening at the movies might cost $2.00 cash and B$4.00 for the ticket, and maybe half cash and half B$ for the refreshments; in contrast, a $100.00 bag of groceries might cost $95.00 cash and B$5.00; a flight from Minneapolis to New York City might cost $175.00 cash and B$175.00; while tuition and books for a semester of college might cost $500.00 cash and B$1500.00.

As the dual currency system matures, every imaginable product or service would become available on a part cash and part Business Incentive Dollar basis. The need for charitable and government programs for needy people could certainly decline, because more and more individuals and their families would enjoy greater purchasing power as well as greater job security.

How Would Decisions Be Made in a Dual Currency Business Alliance?

A dual currency business alliance would operate much like the VISA system, which is cooperatively owned and operated by member banks. The banks control the organization and its operations through representative boards and hired staffs. Each individual bank remains free to run its own affairs and manage its own portfolio of VISA cardholders. The primary difference would be that a dcba would include employers and retailers, as well as banks and transaction companies.

It is important to note that most decisions in a dual currency network would look the same as they do today. Business owners and managers would still make decisions related to prices, employees, cash compensation, as well as how to distribute cash profits. The market would still determine prices, although there would be a second factor for consumers to consider; "What portion B$ can I pay?" Individuals would still decide where to work, as well as how and where to spend their paychecks. Dividends received in B$ would of course be spent only within the dual-currency system. Labor unions would still play their traditional role, although labor-management cooperation might be enhanced through creating a bigger economic pie. Finally, dissatisfied customers would have the exact same recourse under the law that they have today.

The alliance would keep track of and advertise available products and services, manage the dual currency pricing, accounting, and transaction settlement system, determine dividend levels, adjust transaction procedures, and maintain system integrity—much the way that VISA does for its bank membership. Virtually the entire transaction process would be automated and hassle free—simply swipe and sign the dc-card. The dual currency technology checks balances, approves transactions, credits and debits cash and B$ to and from dc-bank accounts, sends dc-statements to merchants and cardholders, and monitors overall system performance.

Benefits to Stakeholders

Dual currency commerce offers numerous benefits to the banking and transaction industry and its stakeholders:

For Retailers and Employers:

- Greater sales and profits and an excellent public relations vehicle.
- Reduced marketing and transaction processing costs for merchants.
- Greater convenience for merchants and consumers through elimination of cash, checks, discount coupons, and proprietary point programs.
- A powerful recruitment and retention tool for employers; improved employee compensation combined with lower labor costs.

For Consumers and Communities:
- Increased purchasing power for cardholders who may be employees, consumers, corporate shareholders, community volunteers, or government benefit recipients.
- New economic resources for communities without resorting to tax or charitable dollars.

For Banks and Transaction Companies:
- Increased revenues for transaction companies and banks. Additional customers for bank card products. New demographic information to capture, process, and sell.
- Participation in a proprietary type of "float."
- Community Reinvestment Act credit from an innovative model of community development.

Key Distinctions of dc-commerce

In summary, there are four key distinctions of dual currency commerce:

- A Unique Market Analysis: A high-tech economy using

knowledge-based resources requires new tools and different rules from an economy based upon scarce material resources. Today, there is a large and growing gap between the productive capabilities of businesses and the purchasing power of most consumers. Increasing consumer purchasing power with a new financial instrument offers a significant business opportunity to the banking and transaction industry..

- A Proprietary Financial Instrument: A new supplemental currency has been designed that can elevate commerce to higher levels of productivity and profitability than what dollars alone make possible. The new currency—a virtual corporate discount scrip—blends the best features of U.S. dollars, discounts, barter dollars, corporate scrip, and service credits.
- A Patented Transaction System: The dual currency transaction system creates a seamless interface between dollars and the new currency. The system manages any two-currency transactions, combining cash with barter dollars, frequent flyer miles, Business Incentive Dollars, or Community Service Credits. Integrating dollars which favor economic competition with a second currency that promotes greater cooperation brings a new win-win dynamic to traditional free enterprise commerce.
- A Dual Currency Business Alliance (DCBA): The DCBA is similar to a strategic business alliance which uses frequent flyer miles as a marketing tool. It is managed like the VISA system through representative boards and hired staffs. The DCBA includes employers, retailers, employees, and consumers, as well as banks and transaction companies.

Incentives for Participation

Unquestionably, there would be many risks for early adopters of dual currency commerce. Most likely, potential rewards are in proportion to those risks. What could motivate leaders of the banking and transaction industry to invest time, talent, and financial resources to develop and test dc-commerce? Simply put, financial gain and altruism.

The market for dc-commerce is businesses the world over that

Deathly Documents

seek more customers, as well as consumers the world over who desire a higher standard of living. How much more of a profit motive could there be?

At the same time, dc-commerce provides a unique opportunity for banks and transaction companies to do what they do best—facilitate bigger, faster, more numerous, and more secure electronic transactions—but in doing so, to leave a legacy that truly honors the power and scope of their industry and gives wings to the highest aspirations of the human spirit.

It is encouraging to observe an entire dual currency industry on the horizon: A dual currency system to dispense cash and food stamp benefits to government clients is already established across the country. The system known as Electronic Benefit Transfer or EBT accesses two separate bank accounts from a single debit card to pay for items in either cash or food stamps. EBT demonstrates that existing banking and transaction systems can easily settle noncash transactions denominated in dollars. As well, the first inkling of dual currency pricing is now appearing in the airlines industry, with special offers for airlines tickets on a part-cash and part-frequent flyer miles basis. Oftentimes, the larger trades in the commercial barter industry are made on a part-cash, part-barter basis, and these will likely become automated just the way that full barter transactions are today.

In Minneapolis, Minnesota, a demonstration project by a company called Commonweal, Inc., is underway utilizing a dual currency cash and Community Service Dollar system to reward youth volunteers for work in their communities. The Commonweal HeroCard Program is the first known case of a system to settle transactions for items priced in two currencies. It has broad backing from local business, community, and government organizations. Lastly, the newly integrated economies of the European Economic Community provide a perfect application for dc-commerce, where products and services could be priced partly in a national currency and partly in ECUs, the new common European currency.

In Conclusion

There is nothing small or simple about introducing a new currency. Yet there is no obstacle that has not already been overcome at some time or other in banking history. Thousands of the first banks failed during the introduction of paper currency— but committed people solved the problems and built the industry. Bank of America and others lost hundreds of millions of dollars in the early years of the credit card industry—an amount recouped hundreds of times over since then. Banking laws, tax laws, and labor laws have continuously been adapted or new ones introduced throughout the history of modern commerce.

The odds are in favor of dual currency commerce, because of the indisputable reality of underutilized business capacity, side by side with extensive unmet consumer and community needs. It is primarily a matter of seeing and seizing the business opportunity. In fact, the required financial resources are likely to be a small fraction of the billions already invested to develop electronic commerce . . . or the trillions spent annually on traditional business competition . . . or the ever growing government and nonprofit expenditures on individuals, families, and communities in economic distress.

The story is told that Henry Ford doubled the wages of his employees, so that they could afford to purchase his Model-T Ford—an unequivocal win-win proposition for the company and its workers. Slightly better known is the legacy of the Carnegie family in building a network of public libraries across the land, when education beyond the grade school level was still a privilege for the upper classes. That legacy benefits thousands of communities and millions of people to this day.

How much greater could be the legacy of the banking and transaction industry, arguably the most powerful institution in the history of the human race? With a little imagination and a little courage, we could find out.

The Human Genome

Welcome to the science of genetics! A vitally important field of knowledge at the foundation of every living thing on earth that it's possible to go through life caring absolutely nothing about. Plumb the depths of your indifference with this elaborate discourse on the human genome. Ⓨ

The Recipe for Life

For all the diversity of the world's five and a half billion people, full of creativity and contradictions, the machinery of every human mind and body is built and run with fewer than 100,000 kinds of protein molecules. And for each of these proteins, we can imagine a single corresponding gene (though there is sometimes some redundancy) whose job it is to ensure an adequate and timely supply. In a material sense, then, all of the subtlety of our species, all of our art and science, is ultimately accounted for by a surprisingly small set of discrete genetic instructions. More surprising still, the differences between two unrelated individuals, between the man next door and Mozart, may reflect a mere handful of differences in their genomic recipes—perhaps one altered word in five hundred. We are far more alike than we are different. At the same time, there is room for near-infinite variety.

It is no overstatement to say that to decode our 100,000 genes in some fundamental way would be an epochal step toward unraveling the manifold mysteries of life.

Some definitions

The human genome is the full complement of genetic material in a human cell. (Despite five and a half billion variations on a theme, the differences from one genome to the next are minute; hence, we hear about the human genome—as if there were only one.) The genome, in turn, is distributed among 23 sets of chromosomes, which, in each of us, have been replicated and re-replicated since the fusion of sperm and egg that marked our conception. The source of our personal uniqueness, our full genome, is therefore preserved in each of our body's several trillion cells. At a more basic level, the genome is DNA, deoxyribonucleic acid, a natural polymer built up of repeating nucleotides, each consisting of a simple sugar, a phosphate group, and one of four nitrogenous bases. In the chromosomes, two DNA strands are twisted together into an entwined spiral—the famous double helix—held together by weak bonds between complementary bases, adenine (A) in one strand to thymine (T) in the other, and cytosine to guanine (C-G). In the language of molecular genetics, each of these linkages constitutes a base pair. All told, if we count only one of each pair of chromosomes, the human genome comprises about three billion base pairs.

The specificity of these base-pair linkages underlies all that is wonderful about DNA. First, replication becomes straightforward. Unzipping the double helix provides unambiguous templates for the synthesis of daughter molecules: One helix begets two with near-perfect fidelity. Second, by a similar template-based process, a means is also available for producing a DNA-like messenger to the cell cytoplasm. There, this messenger RNA, the faithful complement of a particular DNA segment, directs the synthesis of a particular protein. Many subtleties are entailed in the synthesis of proteins, but in a schematic sense, the process is elegantly simple.

Every protein is made up of one or more polypeptide chains,

each a series of (typically) several hundred molecules known as amino acids, linked by so-called peptide bonds. Remarkably, only 20 different kinds of amino acids suffice as the building blocks for all human proteins. The synthesis of a protein chain, then, is simply a matter of specifying a particular sequence of amino acids. This is the role of the messenger RNA. (The same nitrogenous bases are at work in RNA as in DNA, except that uracil takes the place of the DNA base thymine.) Each linear sequence of three bases (both in RNA and in DNA) corresponds uniquely to a single amino acid. The RNA sequence AAU thus dictates that the amino acid asparagine should be added to a polypeptide chain, GCA specifies alanine—and so on. A segment of the chromosomal DNA that directs the synthesis of a single type of protein constitutes a single gene.

A plan of action

In 1990 the Department of Energy and the National Institutes of Health developed a joint research plan for their genome programs, outlining specific goals for the ensuing five years. Three years later, emboldened by progress that was on track or even ahead of schedule, the two agencies put forth an updated five-year plan. Improvements in technology, together with the experience of three years, allowed an even more ambitious prospect.

In broad terms, the revised plan includes goals for genetic and physical mapping of the genome, DNA sequencing, identifying and locating genes, and pursuing further developments in technology and informatics. In addition, the plan emphasizes the continuing importance of the ethical, legal, and social implications of genome research, and it underscores the critical roles of scientific training, technology transfer, and public access to research data and materials.

Tedious Tips

Etiquette Survival Quiz

You may be unable to sleep, but that's no excuse for being vulgar about it. Take this handy little quiz to see how well you'd fare with the cream of society (assuming none of you could sleep). Just for fun, try to imagine the place-setting for a six-course midnight supper. You put the fish fork where?

How much do you really know?

1. The difference between Continental and American Style Dining
   a. American style—the knife is used only for cutting and held in the right hand for righthanded people
   b. Continental style—the knife remains in the left hand and the fork in the right for righthanded people
   c. American style—the tines of the fork face downward when bringing food to your mouth

2. When do you place your napkin on your lap?
   a. Immediately after sitting at the table
   b. When your food arrives
   c. After the host or guest of honor

3. Where do you place your napkin when you leave the table during a meal?
    a. The back of your chair
    b. To the left of your plate unfolded
    c. In a heap on the seat of your chair

4. When dining in someone's home, should you bring your unfinished cocktail to the dinner table?
    a. Never
    b. It is permitted only if the dinner is very informal
    c. If other guests do

5. When seated at a formal table, the only people a guest is required to speak to are his immediate neighbors to the left and right.
    a. True
    b. False

6. What is the customary way to eat soup if served in a bowl without handles?
    a. Lift the rim of the soup plate nearest you at a slight angle while moving your spoon away from you
    b. Pick up and drink from the bowl
    c. Tilt soup bowl toward you and lean forward to catch drops

7. Where should the soup spoon be placed when finished?
    a. On the table
    b. In the soup bowl
    c. On the under plate

8. It's acceptable to rest one's arm on the table when eating.
    a. True
    b. False

9. Eating Continental style, the wrist may rest on the table's edge.
      a. True
      b. False

10. You may butter your roll or bread while holding it in your hand.
      a. True
      b. False

11. Is your bread plate the one on the left or the right?
      a. Left
      b. Right

12. If the person seated next to you takes your bread plate, you should
      a. Slap his hand and tell him he took your plate!
      b. Ask the wait person or host discreetly for another bread plate
      c. Let them keep it and take the person's plate seated on your other side

13. If you wish to decline a refill of wine, water or coffee, you would
      a. Simply say "no thank you"
      b. Cover the glass or cup with the palm of your hand
      c. Push your glass or cup away from you

14. If you are attending a very formal dinner with five or more courses and are unsure of the correct fork or knife to use, you should
      a. Discreetly watch and follow the other guests
      b. Ask the host or service person for assistance when each course arrives
      c. Start with the silverware furthest from your plate and work from the outside in

Tedious Tips

15. To signal the wait person that you're finished with your meal, you would
    a. Place your fork and knife together in the center of your plate, fork to the left with tines up
    b. Place your napkin in your plate and push your plate away from the table
    c. Summon the wait person with a clap of your hands or a wave

16. The correct way to eat spaghetti is
    a. Twirl a few strands in the tines of your fork on the edge of your plate
    b. Twirl it into the base of a spoon with your fork
    c. Cut it into small pieces
    d. Slurp it into your mouth

17. When eating hors d'oeuvres with a toothpick, you should leave the toothpick
    a. In the nearest potted plant
    b. Put back on the tray of hors d'oeuvres
    c. In one's napkin or nearby receptacle

18. When hosting a lunch or dinner and giving your order as well as your guest's, how do you indicate what your guest will be having?
    a. Point and say "she'll" or "he'll" have the chicken
    b. The "Lady" or the "Gentleman" would like to have the chicken
    c. "Bill" will have the chicken and "Karen" will have the fish

19. When you are the guest of honor and the toast is to you, you do not take a drink or toast to yourself.
    a. True
    b. False

20. Is it acceptable to use your cellular phone at the table while dining out?
     a. Modern technology vs. Etiquette does not apply any longer
     b. Leave your cellular phone in the car: they are out of place unless you are a physician on call or have a major business emergency
     c. It is acceptable if you do not speak loudly

Etiquette Survival Quiz Scoring
Give yourself 5 points for every correct answer
   ANSWER KEY: 1-a; 2-c; 3-b; 4-b; 5-a; 6-a; 7-c; 8-b; 9-a; 10-b; 11-a; 12-b; 13-a; 14-c; 15-a; 16-a; 17-c; 18-b; 19-a; 20-b

Understanding Your Score
   20-44 Points—You are very rude and unmannerly. You should definitely not attend formal dinner parties, as you are bound to embarrass yourself and others. Eat at McDonalds or Taco Bell until you can figure out how to be a decent human being who is fit for elegant company.
   45-69 Points—Your etiquette could use some work. You're not exactly ready to dine at the White House, but you could probably manage a casual barbecue, as long as you keep plenty of napkins in your pocket and wear a bib. Practice, practice, practice.
   70-99 Points—You are the perfect guest—a highly desirable dining companion and the envy of princes, politicians, and people who just have a lot of money to blow so they give lavish parties with rumaki and crepes suzette.

Sleepercize

Try to recall the most boring dinner party you've ever attended. Remember every single person who was there. Try to recreate the exact seating arrangement. Now, think back to the actual conversation. What was the topic? Did you contribute? Did any one person monopolize the conversation? What did you wish you were doing instead? How many of the previous rules of etiquette do you recall violating?

Tedious Tips

Alien Abduction

It's so completely bizarre, it has to be true, right? You might have thought that contact with beings from other planets would be a memorable experience, but to judge from this account, you'd be wrong. It's possible the aliens felt the same sense of let-down. If this doesn't send you to dreamland, tune in to Art Bell, broadcasting from Roswell. Ⓨ

First Sight

One day, in 1994, I was on my way home from doing grocery shopping. It was a sunny and clear afternoon. I traveled the highway which went by our home, and was almost there when I suddenly hit traffic. This had never happened before in the last two years we'd lived there; like I said, this road was not a busy one. But there were at least ten cars in front of me, each at a dead stop. As I did the same, I noticed sunlight bouncing off of something in the sky. Above and ahead of me there was a disk shaped object; I could see it quite clearly, even the metal it was made of—which resembled polished aluminum. It seemed to be completely immobile on the sky, and I tried to figure out what it could be. As "flying saucers" had never been of any interest to me, that was not my first thought! I racked my brain trying to remember what different kind new military aircraft existed, that might resemble what I was seeing (especially since this area was constantly used for military exercises, we had jets and helicopters over the house every day). I thought I might be seeing one from behind. As the time passed, though, it became obvious that this thing was not moving away at all. I still kept searching my mind for a military aircraft that was capable of such a feat, besides a helicopter, which it obviously was not. Besides, even a helicopter can't sit that still! I'm not sure how much time passed, my memory feels fuzzy there, a sort of feeling I've experienced many times since, which leads me to suspect a possible abduction took place then. At any rate, the disc did begin to move at some point, and wiped away all my hopes of finding a rational explanation. It went up and down, tilted one way and the other, in precise, jerky movements; then suddenly flew off over the mountains at a speed that caused me to lose my breath! I knew at that moment that what I had just witnessed was not of this world at all. Since then I have continued to study the flight of all man-made aircraft, even birds, anything in the sky, and have not yet found anything capable of maneuvers like I saw that day. When the thing left, it went at an extremely high speed, and, most importantly, did not start at a lower speed and accelerate! If there had been humans inside that thing at that moment, they would have been puréed!

As soon as it was gone, all the cars then began to move. I felt calm and happy, and just returned home. While unpacking groceries with my husband, I off-handedly mentioned that I'd seen something that seemed to be a U.F.O., quickly recounted what happened, then just forgot about the incident entirely.

It wasn't until much later, more than a year, when other things began to happen that I realized the absurdness of my reaction at that time. If, before that incident, someone handed me that situation hypothetically and asked how I would react, the answer would have been simple: I would get out, run to the car ahead of me and ask them if they saw the same thing as I, take down some names and phone numbers, then report the whole thing to the closest police officer. I would have expected to feel a little more perturbed by seeing something that I had always believed did not exist! And why were those cars stopped anyway? Did they stop to observe it too? Many years later I found a book on this subject, and read that sometimes in the presence of these kind of U.F.O.s, car engines stall. I don't remember if that was the case for my car, but I wonder....

For a few weeks after my eyes burned and watered, and I began to have blurred vision when looking at things as far as across my living room. It was then also that I began to have migraines, which we eventually learned were caused by sinus problems. I still did not link any of this to what had transpired that spring day.

The Return

One year later, my youngest son was three months old, and I had not thought about the previous year's sighting at all. Things were going well for us: we had built a new house, with our children's school directly across the street, and I was making friends in the neighborhood. I'd actually never been so content in France, as I could finally speak French enough to feel a part of the community. By that time the strange phenomena in the home had stopped. I had discontinued my relaxation sessions, and things were quite normal. It was in March that I began to get a creepy feeling in the pit of my stomach, that I began to feel anxious, started feeling a bit paranoid, watching out the windows, not knowing what I was looking for. I began to get the feeling that something was coming for me, that I had been told in advance of this planned arrival, indeed, as if I had somehow agreed to a meeting, a long time ago! I began to be terrified of the night. One night there was a program on T.V., a debate about the famous Roswell autopsy film, which I had not heard about until then (apparently the French are much more reluctant than the Americans to consider such phenomena). The subject though seemed to hit a nerve in me, and it was as if I suddenly remembered something that I'd been trying to repress; it was unclear though, something pertaining to D.N.A., I had agreed to help someone. I couldn't get a clear picture in my head, but I knew that that someone was not human, and the U.F.O. was connected. With dread, I had to face that I'd promised to give a sample of D.N.A., for reproductive uses. I had the feeling that I'd agreed because it was a race that needed help, and I felt sorry for them. This did not ease my fear, but made it grow. I was imagining that they might hurt me, begging them silently, not to come, not to hurt me. I could not turn the lights off at night, and had a hell of a time trying to explain that to my husband! I could not tell a soul how terrified I'd become, I was not at all sure that I was not just plain crazy!

For two nights I felt/heard a very low vibration, which seemed to affect me right down to my bones. My husband and I searched everywhere to find the source, thinking that perhaps our new house had not been wired properly, but he could not hear it, and I could not find where it was coming from. Then the night came which finally put an end to my apprehension.

My son was still breastfeeding at the time, which I had done with each of my children for their first year. Any woman who has done that for three kids knows that during that time, she does not sleep heavily. Breastfeeding "on demand" means just that: night or day, when the child calls, she must be able to awake fully and immediately, and not be fuzzy-headed, to avoid putting the baby in the cupboard or nursing the cat! So such was my habit, nocturnal activities were often, and never did I forget what I had done in the night, or even been unclear about it. This, I feel, is important to point out. I cannot say the same is true for me now, I've gotten used to getting a good night's sleep; but at that time, this was not the case.

In the night I had gotten my son out of his room and brought him into our bed to nurse; afterwards, we had fallen asleep. At some point I awoke to feel him slipping away from me, off my arm, towards the edge of the bed. He was not awake and was not squirming at all, just sliding away smoothly as if being pulled by someone. I immediately pulled him back to me and looked around the room, but saw no one. Then I felt myself become almost completely paralyzed, and began to levitate off the bed! As I rose, I began screaming, and clawing at my husband's back to wake him, but he did not awake. When I was roughly two feet off the bed, everything went black. I don't mean to say my memory is sort of unclear about what happened next, or that I just drifted off to sleep; I mean it was a quick and brutal cutting off of consciousness—as if a black curtain had been dropped over my mind.

The next thing I knew, I was waking up, it was morning, and my son was in his bed, although I had no memory of putting him back! I felt strangely content, happy almost, even though I remembered what had happened in my bed. I went into the bathroom and saw immediately a tuft of hair cut off cleanly on the top of my head. I almost laughed out loud when I realized that that was how they took the D.N.A., and I'd been afraid of so much worse! I felt relieved that it was over, and all anxiety was gone. I had that hair sticking up on the top of my head (very noticeable since the rest is very long) for a long time and people often asked what happened...all I could say was, "I don't know." That was the truth, because really, I still thought I might just have been nuts!

Sleepercize

Sing to yourself:
99 little green men on a ship
99 little green men
If one of those aliens happens to flip
98 little green men on a ship.
98 little green men on a ship
98 little green men
If one of those aliens happens to flip
*97 little green men on a ship**
*You know how the rest goes.

Periodontitis

Yes, you may sleep, but dental plaque is always at work, inching you closer to the heartbreak of periodontal disease. You may want to keep a loaded toothbrush on the nightstand in case of unexpected awakenings: at least that way you'll have something to do while you wait to fall asleep again. By the way, it is not advisable to go to sleep with the toothbrush in your mouth. ⓨ

PERIODONTITIS OCCURS WHEN the inflammation of the gums progresses into the deeper underlying structures and bone.

- In the most common form of periodontitis, plaque (and sometimes calculus) is found below the gumline.
- The gums may feel irritated, appear bright red, and bleed easily.
- The ligaments holding the tooth in its socket break down and the gums pull away from the teeth, resulting in a periodontal pocket or space between the tooth and gum.
- The periodontal pocket deepens and fills with more bacteria. Supportive ligaments and bone start to show damage.

Moderate periodontal disease: notice the accumulation of calculus around the gumline. The gums are red, swollen, and tender.

Calculus and plaque do not have to be evident to the naked eye for periodontal disease to be present. You need regular examinations performed by your oral health professional to assess your periodontal health and determine if periodontal disease is active in your mouth.

After non-surgical periodontal therapy (i.e. scaling) the gums have been restored to health. Notice the gums have receded, exposing the root of the tooth. This is due to the irreversible bone loss as result of previous periodontal disease. This can lead to tooth sensitivity.

Advanced Periodontitis
When periodontitis progresses to the advanced stage, the gums severely recede (pull away from the tooth); pockets deepen and may be filled with pus.

In the broadest sense, periodontal disease can be considered any form of ill health affecting the periodontium—the tissues that surround and support the teeth.

These include the gums (or gingiva), the bone of the tooth socket, and the periodontal ligament, a thin layer of connective tissue that holds the tooth in its socket and acts as a cushion between tooth and bone.

Inflammation or infection of the gums is called gingivitis; that of the bone, periodontitis. These conditions can arise for a variety of reasons.

A severe deficiency of vitamin C can lead to scurvy and result in bleeding, spongy gums, and eventual tooth loss. And at least one periodontal disease—the uncommon but highly destructive juvenile periodontitis—is thought to have a strong genetic basis.

But as the terms periodontal disease, gingivitis, and periodontitis are most commonly used, they refer to disease that is caused by the buildup of dental plaque.

Plaque is a combination of bacteria and sticky bacterial products that form on the teeth within hours of cleaning. Its source is the natural bacteria in the mouth, of which more than 300 different species have been identified.

In small amounts and when newly formed, plaque is invisible and relatively harmless. But when left to accumulate, it increases in volume (in large amounts, plaque can be seen as a soft whitish deposit), and the proportion of harmful species in the plaque grows.

Separating Gingivitis

The role played by plaque in the development of gingivitis was demonstrated in the early 1960s. Dental researchers had people stop brushing their teeth and let the plaque in their mouths build up.

Within two to three weeks signs of inflammation appeared—redness, swelling, and an increased tendency to bleed—and when brushing resumed, the inflammation went away.

Gingivitis is fairly common. Just about everybody has it in some degree. A nationwide survey by the National Institute of Dental Research, for example, found that 40 to 50 percent of the adults studied had at least one spot on their gums with inflammation that was prone to bleeding.

At one time gingivitis and periodontitis were thought to be different phases of the same disease, meaning that the sort of inflammation detected in this study would lead inevitably to periodontitis if left untreated.

Yet, many dental researchers no longer believe this to be true. Studies have led dental researchers to two conclusions. One is that gingivitis and periodontitis are different disease entities. And, two, gingivitis is not a particularly serious disease.

Some people with gingivitis do, nonetheless, develop periodontitis. The plaque that causes gingivitis is located at or above the gum line and is referred to as supragingival plaque.

With time, areas of supragingival plaque can become covered by swollen gum tissue or otherwise spread below the gum line (where it is called subgingival plaque), and in this airless environment the harmful bacteria within the plaque proliferate.

These bacteria can injure tissues through the direct secretion

Your Boring Body

of toxins. But they cause the greatest damage by stimulating a chronic inflammatory response in which the body in essence turns on itself, and the periodontal ligament and bone of the tooth socket are broken down and destroyed.

This is similar to what happens in arthritis and, like rheumatoid arthritis, periodontitis is now considered primarily an inflammatory disease.

The bone destruction from periodontitis can be fairly even, resulting in receding gum lines. But more often it causes deep crevices between an individual tooth and its socket.

These crevices are called periodontal pockets, and, just as it once was thought that gingivitis inexorably progressed to periodontitis, so it was once believed that shallow periodontal pockets inevitably deepened, eventually becoming deep enough to jeopardize the socket's support of the adjacent tooth.

Dental researchers, however, have collected substantial evidence to support a theory called the burst hypothesis. This theory states that periodontal bone loss is not a steady process but results instead from periodic flare-ups of infection and inflammatory response inside the pocket.

This theory helps explain epidemiological and clinical findings that many, if not most, periodontal pockets are not actively diseased.

Rather, they are remnants of past infections that the body has overcome. Further, not all periodontal pockets inevitably deepen —some apparently partially heal and get shallower.

What triggers a destructive "burst" inside a periodontal pocket (or, for that matter, the transition from gingivitis to periodontitis) is unknown.

But, as described by these British researchers, such events are most likely the result of unfavorable fluctuations in the balance between the type, quantity and location of bacteria in a person's mouth, the ability to resist bacterial infection, and the unique characteristics of an individual's inflammatory response.

Good News-Bad News
All this has something of a good news-bad news flavor to it. The

good news is that most of us have less to fear than we may have been led to believe.

Periodontal disease is often described as almost universal—a disease that can or will affect almost everyone and that can have "devastating" results.

But most such statements are based on studies that are not only old (dating from the 1950s and early '60s) but that also combine gingivitis and periodontitis under the single heading "periodontal disease."

More recent studies suggest that only about 10 percent of adults have periodontitis severe enough to possibly cause tooth loss. The percentage is lower in younger people and higher in older people. Even among these people it is unusual to have more than a few affected teeth.

The "bad" news generated by all this new research into the causes and natural history of the periodontal diseases (as gingivitis and periodontitis are now referred to collectively) is that while most of us may be at lower risk than previously thought, it is still impossible to say who is at high or low risk individually.

It can't be predicted who with gingivitis will develop periodontitis or who with shallow periodontal pockets will go on to develop deep pockets and possibly lose teeth.

Researchers are, however, working rapidly on methods to make such predictions. These techniques will involve tests of immune function and the types of bacteria in a person's mouth. Once available, they are expected to dramatically change current approaches to the treatment of periodontitis.

Today, periodontitis is treated either by surgically eliminating periodontal pockets or by cleaning affected tooth roots in a process known as scaling and planing. The current trend is towards the latter, and the ability to predict who is susceptible to worsening disease could accelerate the move in this direction.

By one estimate, such predictions could make 90 percent of "pocket elimination" surgeries unnecessary.

Your Boring Body

The Perfect Cup of Coffee

There's no better way of enticing sleep than by imagining what you'll drink first thing in the morning. Only what kind of coffee is right for you? One coffee roaster has generously compiled this coffee profiler to clear up the question of what blend belongs in your cup. After going through this several times, you'll need it. Ⓨ

NEED HELP CHOOSING the perfect coffee?

We can match your tastes to the coffee type right for you! First, answer the questions below. Then total the number of answers in each column. The column with the most answers identifies the coffees most suited to your tastes.

What flavors do you prefer?	nutty	fruity	spicy	sweet
How do you prefer your steak?	rare	medium rare	medium well	well done
Which fruit do you prefer?	grapefruit	orange	melon	banana
How do you like marshmallows?	white	golden brown	—burned—	
Which chocolate is your favorite?	—milk—		—dark—	
Which grapes do you prefer?	—white—		—red—	
What wine do you prefer?	dry white	sweet white	light-body red	heavy-body red
Total # of answers in each column				
	if you had the most answers in this column try these coffees	if you had the most answers in this column try these coffees	if you had the most answers in this column try these coffees	if you had the most answers in this column try these coffees
Taste Bud Type™	Clean & Simple	Brisk & Bright	Sweet & Balanced	Decadent & Smooth

Coffee Types by "Taste Bud Type™"

Clean & Simple	Brisk & Bright	Sweet & Balanced	Decadent & Smooth
Coffee House Blend	Daybreak Morning	Caribou Blend	Fireside Evening
New Guinea	Colombia	Guatemala	French Roast
Kona Blend	Roastmaster's Blend	Kenya AA	Sumatra
Wilderness Blend	La Minita Peaberry	Costa Rica	Espresso
	Ethiopia		Caribou Blend Dark
			Kenya AA Dark
			Costa Rica Dark

Sleepercize

Go through the past three days in your mind. Think of every cup of coffee you've had. Picture the actual scenes. Were you alone? At work? With a friend? What were you doing while you were drinking each coffee? What were you talking about? Thinking about? (You absolutely may *not* have any coffee right now!)

Tedious Tips

Flight Safety Instructions

Ever wondered what happens to the flight crew shortly after going through the flight safety instructions? They crawl away to sleep it off! Prepare the cabin for take-off, strap yourself in, and get ready for a non-stop flight to Dreamland. ☉

747/DC10/757

Welcome

Ladies and gentlemen. Welcome onboard Northwest Airlines to [with continuing service to _____]. My name is _____ and I am the lead flight attendant.

[International Flights with Interpreter] Our interpreter(s) is/are _____ who speak(s) _____ and _____.

[Interport Flights with Main Cabin Lead] The main cabin lead flight attendant is _____.

[747 and DC10] The main cabin coordinator is _____.

Safety Video

[If video is inoperative, refer to "Inoperative Safety Video."]

Please direct your attention to the video screens [and monitors] for important safety information. There is an instruction card in your seat pocket that illustrates the safety equipment on this aircraft.

U.S. federal regulations require compliance with this information as well as all crew instructions, lighted information signs, and posted placards.

[Show video]

[In addition to the equipment shown in the video, a life raft is located in a ceiling panel above the right overwing exit.]

Cabin lights will now be turned off. Reading light buttons are located (above your seat/in the armrest of your seat). Thank you for your attention.

Inoperative Safety Video

At this time, please direct your attention to the cabin crew for important safety information. There is an instruction card in your seat pocket that illustrates the safety equipment on this aircraft.

U.S. federal regulations require compliance with this information as well as all crew instructions, lighted information signs, and posted placards.

Seat Belts

Fasten your seat belt by inserting the metal tip into the buckle. Tighten by pulling on the belt. To unfasten your seat belt, lift the metal flap on the buckle. It is Northwest Airlines' policy that you keep your seat belts fastened at all times while seated.

Exits/Slides/Rafts

[747]

This aircraft has five doors on each side of the main deck.

- [747-100/200] An additional exit located in the upper deck is only used when directed by a crew member.
- [747-400] Two additional doors are located in the upper deck.

Slides may be detached and used as life rafts except at the upper deck and overwing doors.

Tedious Tips

- [747-100] An additional life raft is located in a ceiling panel above the right overwing exit.

[DC10]

This aircraft has four doors on each side.

Each door is equipped with a slide that may be detached and used as a life raft.

[757]

- [757-5500] This aircraft has four doors on each side. Each door is equipped with a slide that may be detached and used as a flotation device.
- [757-5600] This aircraft has three door and two window exits on each side. Window exits lead to off-wing slides. To operate, remove the handle cover and pull the handle down and in. Slides may be detached and used as flotation devices, except those over the wings.

Doors are clearly marked with exit signs and instructions for door operation. Each door is equipped with an escape slide.

Locate the exit nearest to you. The nearest exit may be behind.

Emergency Path Lights

In an emergency, white lights illuminate the aisles.

Oxygen

The cabin is pressurized. If there is a loss of cabin pressure, a panel above you will open and an oxygen mask will drop.

Remain seated with your seat belt fastened and pull the mask toward you to start the flow of oxygen. Oxygen will be flowing to the mask even though the bag may not inflate.

Cover your nose and mouth with the mask. Place the elastic band around your head and tighten by pulling on the ends. Secure your own mask before assisting others.

Flotation Devices

Your seat bottom cushion may be used as a flotation device. Pull up and remove the cushion. Put your arms through the straps at the bottom and hold the cushion to your chest.

[Life Vest–Equipped Aircraft]

[Overwater: Read and perform demo; Non-overwater: Read announcement only]

In addition, a life vest is located in a pouch beneath your seat.

In a water evacuation, remove the vest from the pouch, throw the flap over your shoulder, and pull the vest over your head. Secure the straps around your waist. Do not inflate the vest until you leave the aircraft.

Pull down on the red tabs in front to automatically inflate your vest. To manually inflate, blow into the tubes on either side. A water-activated light is attached to each vest.

Conclusion

Cabin lights will now be turned off. Reading light buttons are located (above your seat/in the armrest of your seat). Thank you for your attention.

Tedious Tips

What do *you* do
when you can't sleep?
Do you have any hot tips
for insomniacs?

Share with us by going to
the YAWN! web page
at Ten Speed Press's web site:
www.tenspeed.com

Permissions

"Elvis Meets Nixon" contains Presley's letter to President Nixon as recorded in the *National Archives and Records Administration:* http://www.nara.gov/exhall/nixonelvis/letter.html.

"Stain Removal Guide" was revised by Dr. Everlyn S. Johnson and can be found on the Mississippi State Extension Service: http://ext.msstate.edu/pubs/pub1400.htm

"How to Get a Good Night's Sleep" is taken from Tamar Nordenberg's *Tossing and Turning No More: How to Get a Good Night's Sleep* published in FDA Consumer Magazine (July-August 1998) found online at: http://www.fda.gov/fdac/features/1998/498_sleep.html.

"Dietary Fiber" is excerpted from Fiber: *Byerly's Shopping For Your Health,* © 1996 Byerly's, a subsidiary of Lund Food Holdings, Inc. Reprinted by permission of Lund Food Holdings, Inc.

"Sea Turtles" is taken from the article *NOAA Fisheries and U.S. Fish and Wildlife Service Join Forces to Help Save Sea Turtles,* found on *NOAA News Online (Story 265):* http://www.yoto98.noaa.gov/books/turtles/turtle1.htm.

"Genesis 36" Scripture taken from *The Holy Bible, New International Version,* © 1973, 1978, 1884 by International Bible Society. Used by permission of Zondervan Publishing House.

"President Clinton's Grand Jury Testimony" is taken from Court TV Online, © 1999 by the Courtroom Television Network LLC. All rights reserved. http://www.courttv.com/casefiles/clintoncrisis/.

"Taming the Paper Trail" is an article from NAPSI's *Managing Your Office,* found at: http://www.napsnet.com/envir/42776.html.

"The Declaration of Independence" found on the National Archives and Record Administration's website at http://www.nara.gov/exhall/charters/declaration

"Hair Loss" is taken from Devera Pine's *From Personal Statement to Personal Problem,* found at *FDA/CESAN Cosmetics:* http://www.vm.cfsan.fda.gov/~dms/cos-817.html.

"Golf Strategies" is taken from NAPSI's *Strategies For Changing Conditions,* by Dr. Craig Farnsworth. The North American Precis Syndicate, Inc. address is: http://www.napsnet.com/.

"Exodus 22" is taken from *The Holy Bible, King James Version.*

"Can Insomnia Affect Your Quality of Life?" is from NAPSI's *Spotlight on Health.* The North American Precis Syndicate, Inc. address is: http://www.napsnet.com/

"Snow and Ice Control" is taken from *More Efficient Winter Operation,* found on RoadSavers web site: http://www.ota.fhwa.dot.gov/roadsvr/icebro.htm.

"Nutrition Guidelines" was originally adapted from Pate, et al., *Journal of the American Medical Association,* © 1995, Vol. 273, p. 404.

"NASA Fatigue Countermeasures" is taken from NASA's webpage *Fatigue Countermeasures Program,* curated by Ray Oyung. Found at: http://www-afo.arc.nasa.gov/zteam/.

"Practical Palmistry" is excerpted from Eveline Michell Farwell's *Practical Palmistry for the Amateur,* published by The Page Company, Boston, © 1917.

"John Glenn's 'Friendship 7' Transcript" is found in the *Records of the National Aeronautics and Space Administration of the National Archives and Records Administration,* Southwest Region (Fort Worth, Texas) at: http://www.nara.gov/exhall/glenn/trnscrpt.html.

"The Asian Longhorn Beetle" is taken from the Minnesota Department of Agriculture's *Asian Longhorn Beetle Alert* web page at http://www.mda.state.mi.us/hot/asianbeetle.

"Air Bag Safety" Appendix A—Information Brochure is found on the National Highway Traffic Safety site at : http://nhtsa.gov.

"Ingrown Toenails" is information provided by the American Academy of Family Physicians.

"Dog Training Tips" appears as originally published on CES Dog Training's Web site, *Barking; Jumping; Crate Training,* © 7/26/99. Reprinted by permission of author, CES Dog Training owner, Carmen Strich: http://www.cesdogtraining.com.

"Income Tax Instructions" is adapted from the *1996 Minnesota Individual Income Tax Forms and Instructions,* Minnesota Department of Revenue.

"Halcion Dosage Information" appears as originally published under *Halcion* at Health-Center.com. Reprinted by permission of Health-Center.com: http://www.health-center.com.

"The Story of the Odyssey" is taken from Chapter 12 "The Dwellings of the Dead" from Rev. Alfred J. Church M.A.'s *The Story of the Odyssey,* published by The Macmillan Company, New York, © 1902.

"Lotus Software Agreement" appears as originally published by Lotus Development Corporation. Reprinted by permission of Lotus Development Corporation.

"Vowel Matching" is an original article by Tom Raburn entitled *Let's Talk Craft—Vowel Matching,* © September 1998 Tom Raburn. Found at: http://www.harmonize.com/probe/aids/crafts/vowels.htm

"The Battle of Fort Stephenson" was originally published as *George Croghan and the Battle of Fort Stephenson,* by Jim Dandy Productions, © 1997 Frank Hull Eachus.

"Airline Ticket Fine Print" is taken from Northwest Airlines' *Ticketing Information and Emergency Instruction.* Reprinted by permission of Northwest Airlines.

"Milk Substitutes" is excerpted from *Lactose Intolerance,* © 1992 Byerly's, a subsidiary of Lund Food Holdings, Inc. Reprinted by permission of Lund Food Holdings, Inc.

"Beets" is excerpted from *The Byerly Bag: Versatile Vegetable—Beets,* © 1999 Byerly's, All Rights Reserved. Reprinted by permission of Lund Food Holdings, Inc.

"Dual Currency Economics" is reprinted by permission of Joel Hodroff who is CEO of dualcurrency Systems, Inc. (dcs) which licenses the use of its patents for dualcurrency pricing, accounting, and transaction settlement systems. He may be contacted at: joelhodroff@dualcurrency.com.

"The Human Genome" is taken from the Human Genome Project Information web site, sponsored by the U.S. Department of Energy Human Genome Program: http://www.ornl.gov/hgmis.

"Etiquette Survival Quiz" was originally created by Sue Fox, Founder of Etiquette Survival, Inc. and reprinted by her permission. Found at: http://www.etiquettesurvival.com.

"Alien Abduction" is adapted from *True Abduction*, © 12/19/98 by an anonymous author, and from Ben Field's *The Roswell Timeline*, © 11/15/99, and reprinted by permission of Ben Field. Both stories may be found at Field's web site: http://www.abcfield.force9.co.uk

"Periodontitis" is excerpted from *Stages of Gum Disease* from The Wisdom Tooth Home Page. Reprinted by permission of The Wisdom Tooth Home Page: http://www.umanitoba.ca/outreach/wisdomtooth/stagesof.htm.

"The Perfect Cup of Coffee" is taken from Caribou Coffee's brochure *Need Help Choosing the Perfect Coffee?* Reprinted by permission of Caribou Coffee.

"Flight Safety Instructions" is taken from Northwest Airlines' *Ticketing Information and Emergency Instruction*. Reprinted by permission of Northwest Airlines.